Personality:
A Cognitive
Approach

'This is an outstanding text on personality which is not only easy to read but also very well structured and written. The chapters on attributions and cognitive styles are particularly significant, and provide added value to more traditional texts.'

Professor Cary L. Cooper, *UMIST*

'A well written book . . . I liked the early emphasis on schools of psychology and the clear exposition of why/when theories of personality developed.'

Professor Colin Cooper, *Queen's University of Belfast*

Are individual differences best explained in terms of nature (biology/genetics) or nurture (upbringing)? Do we have 'free will'? Is personality a result of differences in cognition or differences in temperament? *Personality: A Cognitive Approach* touches on a number of controversies in academic psychology, and provides a broad and eclectic view of individual differences psychology. Jo Brunas-Wagstaff integrates research and theories relevant to the study of human differences from the areas of cognitive psychology, social cognition and applied clinical psychology with 'traditional' personality perspectives to provide a concise yet academically rigorous overview of the area.

Jo Brunas-Wagstaff is Senior Lecturer in Psychology at Liverpool Hope University College.

Psychology Focus

Series editor: Perry Hinton, University of Luton

The Psychology Focus series provides students with a new focus on key topic areas in psychology. It supports students taking modules in psychology, whether for a psychology degree or a combined programme, and those renewing their qualification in a related discipline. Each short book:

- presents clear, in-depth coverage of a discrete area with many applied examples
- assumes no prior knowledge of psychology
- has been written by an experienced teacher
- has chapter summaries, annotated further reading and a glossary of key terms.

Also available in this series:

Friendship in Childhood and Adolescence
Phil Erwin

Gender and Social Psychology
Vivien Burr

Jobs, Technology and People
Nik Chmiel

Learning and Studying
James Hartley

Forthcoming in 1999:

Being Ill
Marian Pitts

Intelligence and Abilities
Colin Cooper

Stress, Cognition and Health
Tony Cassidy

Types of Thinking
Ian Robertson

Personality: A Cognitive Approach

- Jo Brunas-Wagstaff

ROUTLEDGE

LONDON AND NEW YORK

First published in 1998
by Routledge
11 New Fetter Lane, London
EC4P 4EE

Simultaneously published in
the USA and Canada
by Routledge
29 West 35th Street, New York,
NY 10001

© 1998 Jo Brunas-Wagstaff

Typeset in Sabon and Futura by
Florencetype Ltd, Stoodleigh, Devon

Printed and bound in Great Britain by
TJ International Ltd, Padstow,
Cornwall

*British Library Cataloguing in
Publication Data*
A catalogue record for this book is
available from the British Library

*Library of Congress Cataloging in
Publication Data*
Brunas-Wagstaff, Jo, 1961–
Personality : a cognitive approach /
Jo Brunas-Wagstaff.
p. cm. – (Psychology focus)
Includes bibliographical references
and index.
1. Personality. 2. Individual
differences. I. Title. II. Series.
BF698.B73 1998
155.2–dc21   97–39541

ISBN 0–415–16304–8 (hbk)

ISBN 0–415–16305–6 (pbk)

Contents

CONTENTS

Tables

vii

Series preface

The Psychology Focus series provides short, up-to-date accounts of key areas in psychology without assuming the reader's prior knowledge in the subject. Psychology is often a favoured subject area for study, since it is relevant to a wide range of disciplines such as Sociology, Education, Nursing and Business Studies. These relatively inexpensive but focused short texts combine sufficient detail for psychology specialists with sufficient clarity for non-specialists.

The series authors are academics experienced in undergraduate teaching as well as research. Each takes a key topic within their area of psychological expertise and presents a short review, highlighting important themes and including both theory and research findings. Each aspect of the topic is clearly explained with supporting glossaries to elucidate technical terms.

The series has been conceived within the context of the increasing modularisation which has been developed in higher education over the last decade and fulfils the consequent need for clear, focused, topic-based course material. Instead of following one course of study, students on a modularisation programme are often able to choose modules from a wide range of disciplines to complement the modules they are required to study for a specific degree. It can no longer be assumed that students studying a particular module will necessarily have the same background knowledge (or lack of it!) in that subject. But they will need to familiarise themselves with a particular topic since a single module in a single topic may be only 15 weeks long, with assessments arising during that period. They may have to combine eight or more modules in a single year to obtain a degree at the end of their programme of study.

One possible problem with studying a range of separate modules is that the relevance of a particular topic or the relationship between topics may not always be apparent. In the Psychology Focus series authors have drawn where possible on practical and applied examples to support the points being made so that readers can see the wider relevance of the topic under study. Also, the study of psychology is usually broken up into separate areas, such as social psychology, developmental psychology and cognitive psychology, to take three examples. Whilst the books in the Psychology Focus series will provide excellent coverage of certain key topics within these 'traditional' areas, the authors have not been constrained in their examples and explanations and may draw on material across the whole field of psychology to help explain the topic under study more fully.

Each text in the series provides the reader with a range of important material on a specific topic. They are suitably comprehensive and give a clear account of the important issues involved. The authors analyse and interpret the material as well as present an up-to-date and detailed review of key work. Recent references are provided along with suggested further reading to allow readers to investigate the topic in more depth. It is hoped, therefore, that after following the informative review of a key topic in a Psychology Focus text, readers will not only have a clear understanding of the issues in question but will be intrigued and challenged to investigate the topic further.

Acknowledgements

For Graham, Bobby, Toby and Megan.

With grateful thanks to the Management at Liverpool Hope University College and the staff in the Psychology Department for their much valued support while I was writing this book.

Chapter 1

Introduction and overview

Individual differences: the background

Research and theories in psychology have tended to share the broad aim of understanding generalities in human behaviour. Most of psychology is therefore dedicated to explaining what human beings share in common, for example how human behaviour develops from birth to adulthood (developmental psychology); how humans think, process information and solve problems (cognitive psychology); the general rules which govern human social interaction (social psychology), or how our perceptual systems register and interpret information about the world in which we live (the study of human perception). However, although humans are similar in very many ways, one obvious aspect of being human is that we are also individuals. Human beings can differ in their perception of objects and events: for example, two people sitting in the same room may disagree about whether it is too hot or too cold. Differences in how we each think about objects and events are even more apparent: we have different likes and dislikes (different attitudes) and different preferences (we may disagree with each other about the best way to handle a situation or tackle a particular problem). More obvious still are individual differences in behaviour: whereas some of us are sociable and outgoing at a party, others are quiet and withdrawn. Individual differences are therefore as much a part of human nature as similarities between people.

The fact that people differ is one of the first things of which a student of human behaviour is made aware. Strangely enough, however, differences between people are usually introduced to students as an embarrassing problem in psychological research, and the first thing students learn when they begin a psychology course is how to control for differences between people, or how to rule out individual differences, when designing experiments. For example, when designing an experiment to investigate whether people perform better alone than in groups, students are taught early on in their course how to make sure that they use people who are as similar as possible under each condition of the experiment (the alone condition and the in-groups condition), so that differences between people do not influence the outcome of their study. This is perfectly appropriate, of course, if we wish to draw general conclusions about the effects of the presence of others on human performance. However, the tendency to underline the importance of controlling for individual differences in psychology experiments can give students the impression that differences between people are of no interest to psychologists. Consequently, students and psychologists alike often miss out on some very interesting phenomena by approaching the subject only in this way. Suppose that instead of trying to rule out differences between people, we decided to focus on those differences. For example, we could set up a different experiment to look at whether some people perform better in company, whereas others perform better alone. In this way, instead of setting aside differences between people, we could investigate those differences directly and try to explain them. This approach to understanding differences between people (rather than generalities in human nature) is often referred to by psychologists as the study of individual differences. It is possible to study individual differences in relation to any of the phenomena which psychologists typically study, including perception, thinking, problem-solving and social interaction. Strictly speaking, therefore, individual differences psychology is not a single area of psychology, rather it permeates all areas of psychology.

There are a number of alternative ways in which we can explain differences which we observe between people. We can assume that people behave differently to the extent that their behaviour is observed in different situations. Thus person 'x' in company may behave differently from person 'y' when alone. However, this sort of difference would not be a difference between individuals as such, it is a difference between situations. This is not what is meant by an *individual* difference. Anyone's behaviour is different under different circumstances. The real test of an individual difference is when we compare the behaviour of individuals in the same situation. The fact that people do not always behave in the same way in the same situation suggests that, to some extent, differences between people exist separately from the contexts in which their behaviour is observed.

Having acknowledged that individual differences between people can be distinguished from differences between situations in explaining behaviour, we must ask ourselves why one person behaves in one way, whilst another person behaves in a different way in the same situation. There are two possible answers to this question. We could assume that people behave differently because they react to specific situations differently. For instance, 'x' may think of a situation as threatening, whereas 'y' may think the same situation is stimulating or challenging. In this case, whereas we might expect 'x' and 'y''s behaviour always to differ whenever they find themselves in the same situation again, we cannot draw conclusions about the behaviour of 'x' or 'y' in other situations. For all we know, their behaviour may be similar in most other contexts. Alternatively, we could assume that people behave differently because they are different from each other in some fundamental way. In other words, we could assume that the behaviour of 'x' and 'y' usually differs, in most situations. In this case, we need to establish what it is that distinguishes 'x' as a person from 'y' as a person. If we succeed in this we can then try to predict 'x' and 'y''s behaviour across many situations, from a knowledge of their individual characters.

The challenge for researchers in individual differences is therefore to distinguish empirically between these alternative explanations of behavioural differences. Each explanation comes with its associated advantages and disadvantages. For example, it is not always possible to establish whether differences in behaviour are due to situations, or due to something about the person, because we do not usually have the opportunity to observe different people under identical conditions. Even if we were to observe people in the same room, each individual may have a different perspective of events: one may be standing, another sitting; one person may be listening to a conversation which another person cannot hear. Nor can we easily establish whether people behave differently because they think about situations in different ways. Even if we could set up an identical situation in which to observe people, we still would not be able to observe their thoughts about what is going on. If we want to understand how people think differently, we can only infer their thoughts from their behaviour (behaviour here can include a verbal account of what the person is thinking). Finally, if we assume that there are fundamental differences between individuals which influence their behaviour in most situations, we must first discover what those fundamental differences are, and be able to measure them. Furthermore, if human behaviour is deemed primarily to be the result of differences between people, this would appear to deny the importance of situations in influencing behaviour.

However, when most of us talk about differences between people we usually mean that people differ from each other in their behaviour, thoughts and perceptions, in combination, because all of these processes form part of what we think of as a person. Many psychologists use the term 'personality' to describe patterns of perceiving, thinking and behaviour which characterise people. The use of the term 'personality' in psychology is not dissimilar to its use in everyday language as a term to describe collections of ways in which people differ from each other. The label 'personality' can be more useful than the term 'individual differences' because it reflects the popular conception of a person as a unit or 'package'.

In everyday language, the term 'personality' can have a variety of meanings. For example, we may speak of someone we know as having a 'pleasant' or 'unpleasant' personality, we might be more precise and say that they have a 'shy' personality or a 'fun-loving' personality, or we might even describe someone as having 'no personality'. However, if we were asked to define precisely what we mean by 'personality', most of us would not know where to begin; and even if we could be persuaded to attempt a definition, it is unlikely that each of us would come up with exactly the same one. Allport (1937), a personality psychologist, listed fifty different definitions of personality.

On the other hand, the fact that we refer to something called 'personality' at all in everyday language suggests that people must share an understanding of its general meaning, even though we may all be at a loss to define the term precisely. For one thing, we all appear to acknowledge that something called 'personality' exists because we use adjectives to qualify the term. We describe people routinely as having a 'shy' or 'open' personality, and even when we describe someone as having 'no personality' we do not mean this in its literal sense, we merely wish to say that the person we are describing is 'unremarkable'.

Thus, given the use of the term 'personality' in everyday language, we can at least conclude that personality is a collective term which we apply to a 'package' of qualities which people have. Furthermore, the characteristics included under the label 'personality' can qualify people to different extents (to say 'Helen is fun-loving' implies that some other people are not so fun-loving) and when we use labels such as 'shy' or 'fun-loving' to qualify a person, we are suggesting that these characteristics are relatively stable. When someone is described to us as 'shy' we know that we can expect them to be shy most, if not all, of the time.

These conclusions, however, are by no means definitive. After all, it would not be possible to cover every single use of the term 'personality' in everyday language. Nevertheless, some psychologists have reasoned that if our ideas about personality appear to fit those of others, then perhaps we might all agree that together we have come close to an approximate shared concept of 'personality'. Allport followed the same logic when he came up with the following definition of personality, based on his analysis of various definitions of personality from numerous sources: 'Personality is a dynamic organisation, inside the person, of psychophysical systems that create the person's characteristic patterns of behaviour, thoughts and feelings.' (1961: 28).

What is personality psychology?

Personality psychology has therefore emerged as a discipline within mainstream psychology, which attempts to describe and understand what Allport's definition refers to as the 'dynamic organisation, inside the person' of these 'psychophysical systems' or 'characteristic patterns of behaviour, thoughts and feelings'.

It can be noted how Allport's definition is consistent with some of the everyday assumptions that people make about the nature of personality. His definition suggests that 'personality' refers to 'patterns of behaviour' which are 'characteristic' of individuals. In other words, he agrees with the conclusion that personality is a collective term for the qualities that people possess. Also, his use of the term 'characteristic' suggests that he considers that these qualities are possessed to different extents by different people; and the phrase 'patterns of behaviour' would also suggest that he considers personality to be relatively enduring. His definition also covers some aspects of 'personality' which were not included in our initial list of conceptions. He is more precise about the sorts of qualities to which 'personality' might refer: he refers to behaviour, thoughts and feelings. Also, his definition locates 'personality' within the person, and more exactly within 'psychophysical' systems (by this he means that personality may have a basis in the psyche or within our physiology, or both).

Allport and other personality psychologists therefore recognise that people are individuals, and that whatever constitutes this individuality (something labelled 'personality') deserves to be investigated in its own right. However, to say that people have different personalities does not tell us precisely *how* people differ: whether they perceive things differently, think differently, behave differently, or all three. It only implies that they differ in a rather general, abstract way. This means that if we wish to study 'personality' itself, we must agree on which underlying psychological processes (perception, thought or behaviour) are the most important aspects of personality. The fact that personality psychologists themselves cannot always agree on which processes are most important can often be confusing to the student of personality psychology.

However, although personality psychologists disagree about precisely how 'personality' should be defined, they do share one common assumption. They assume that 'personality' is a 'disposition' (i.e. it predisposes the person to think and act in characteristic ways). All personality psychologists therefore attempt to explain individual differences in terms of underlying personality dispositions or temperaments which characterise people, even though they may disagree about how to define personality. For example, those whose performance on a task is improved by the presence of other people may be described by a personality psychologist as having a 'sociable' or 'gregarious' temperament and their improved performance may be explained in terms of their having the kind of personality which allows them to benefit from company in a way which someone who is not sociable or gregarious does not. This level of explanation for someone's performance goes beyond merely describing individual differences in performance on the task as being due to different external events (the presence or absence of others) or even differences in the way people think about the particular task. This is because if we accept that people are characterised by a 'sociable' temperament which influences their behaviour in one situation, then we should also be able to predict that people with a 'sociable' temperament should differ from people who do not have a 'sociable' temperament, across a variety of different social situations. A basic assumption shared by all personality psychologists therefore is that from a knowledge of personality characteristics we should be able to predict how people will behave across a variety of situations. To this end, personality theorists have tried to identify the underlying temperaments, or personality characteristics, which distinguish people from one another and, as personality is an implicit construct (it is unobservable because it resides within us), to develop methods for inferring and measuring those personality characteristics. In contrast, other researchers into individual differences from mainstream psychology have preferred not to invoke temperaments to explain their observations. Instead, they have tended to explain individual differences in behaviour, in terms of differences in basic processes (such as thought or perception) which might underlie how people react to specific situations. An example would be describing the strategies which different people use to remember a list of words. How a person goes about remembering a list of words tells us little, if anything, about their global characteristics, or how they might behave in other situations. However, it does provide us with a detailed insight into that person's behaviour and thought processes in this particular situation.

Understanding individual differences

Psychologists studying individual differences can thus be divided into two broad groups. Personality psychologists, who propose and investigate global theories of human individuality, and psychologists who study individual differences in relation to psychological processes such as social perception, problem-solving, memory or perception within more specific contexts. Studies of personality by personality psychologists and studies of individual differences from within mainstream psychology have thus often tended to proceed in parallel, using alternative methodologies and alternative theoretical perspectives to interpret their findings. However, the view taken in this book is that it may not be fruitful to view these approaches in isolation, rather, that each has much to contribute to an understanding of the other. For instance, recent developments within the mainstream psychological disciplines of social cognition and cognitive psychology have suggested that individual differences in social perception and information processing may offer an alternative way of conceptualising 'personality' in terms of a collection of 'cognitive information processing styles'. Consequently, the book is divided into two main parts. The first considers the traditional personality approach to individual differences and the methodological and theoretical problems associated with defining and measuring personality, while the second part shows how our understanding of personality can be increased and many of the problems resolved by reference to research on individual differences from the broad areas of social and cognitive psychology.

However, whether we prefer to think of individual differences in terms of personality characteristics which determine our behaviour in most situations, or in terms of differences in perception, thought or behaviour in specific situations, ultimately, as psychologists, we would hope to be able to answer questions about how human individuality arises in the first place. For instance, do differences between people ultimately have a biological or social explanation? And are individual differences best explained in terms of cognitive psychological processes (as differences in the ways our minds encode, store or access past experiences), or in terms of physiological processes (differences in the physiology and biochemistry of the brain)? Many of these issues have been hotly debated for centuries by scientists and philosophers, long before psychology emerged as a scientific discipline, and many of the issues have still to be resolved. Chapter 2 therefore outlines some of the issues which have concerned students of personality and individual differences within a historical context, and traces the emergence of personality psychology as a separate discipline within mainstream psychology.

Summary

People clearly differ from each other in the ways in which they perceive events, think and behave. Some psychologists have therefore tried to describe the different psychological processes which might account for individual differences in perception, thought or behaviour in specific situations. However, another way of approaching the study of differences between people is to assume that people differ because they have different characters, personalities or temperaments. This latter approach is known as personality psychology. One aim of personality psychologists is therefore to be able to predict how people will behave in many situations from a knowledge of their personality characteristics. Thus psychologists studying individual differences have tended to focus either on the basic psychological processes which people use to process information within specific contexts, or on trying to identify underlying temperaments or dispositions which characterise people to different extents. The view taken in this book, however, is that the two approaches have much to contribute to each other.

Chapter 2

Personality through history

The lay perspective

Trying to trace the first theories of personality and individual differences is a little like asking when people first began to sleep or eat. Our own observations of people and our expectancies about how people will behave are themselves theories of personality, and have probably been a part of human nature for as long as people have been social beings. Hampson (1988) calls this 'amateur approach to personality psychology ... the Lay Perspective'. For example, when you describe somebody as 'friendly' or 'nervous' you base your description of them on observations you have made of their behaviour. Alternatively, if someone is described to you as 'friendly' or 'nervous' you will have specific expectancies about what they will be like when you do eventually meet them. This everyday process of observation and prediction is not unlike the methods used by social scientists to help them to understand human behaviour. After all, scientific methodology is based on making observations and generating predictions about future events from them. So can personality psychology teach us anything that we do not already know?

However, although social scientists attempt to observe and make predictions about human behaviour, just as the lay person does, a third element is also present in scientific methodology: that of '*systematic* observation'. Everyday observations of behaviour are carried out in a rather unsystematic way. We may conclude that people are 'friendly' or 'nervous' because that is what they are like with us. We do not have the opportunity to observe their behaviour when we are not present. Furthermore, we tend to observe people across a rather limited set of situations, such as at college, at home or at work. Unless we know someone very well indeed, we do not often see them in all situations. Even when we have known someone for years, it is not unusual for us to be surprised by their reactions to some things, and we have all experienced a situation whereby someone we thought was confident and outgoing discloses, when we know them better, that they feel insecure underneath. Of course, a single social scientist does not have access to every behaviour displayed by an individual in every context any more than the lay person has, but the advantage of science is that it relies on multiple observations made across diverse contexts by a variety of researchers. If each of these researchers carries out his/her own observations, and strives to make these as systematic as possible, then we are all on our way towards a more empirical, scientific study of the person in which each set of observations can be verified by others.

Ancient beginnings

Thus, although personality psychology began with lay theories based on simple observations and predictions, over time these have become progressively more systematic. Some of the earliest personality theorists were not psychologists at all, but philosophers. For example, the ancient Greek philosopher, Plato (428–347 BC, 1987), had his own simple theory of personality. He argued that personality is made up of three parts: reason, spirit (vigour or enthusiasm) and desire or appetite. For an individual to be good or just, reason and spirit must be put in charge of appetite, so that appetite can be kept in check. A person whose reason and spirit are in control of his appetite will show characteristics such as 'honesty' 'loyalty' and 'trustworthiness'. On the other hand, a person whose appetite is allowed to predominate will steal, be irreligious and dishonour his parents. In this way, Plato attempted to account for differences between individuals' patterns of behaviour. Plato's pupil, Aristotle (384–322 BC, 1984), on the other hand, argued that differences between individuals arise from a striving towards human excellence. According to Aristotle, excellence belongs to the soul and there are two types of excellence: rational and moral (meaning concerned with character). The moral part is governed by an irrational part of the person which must become obedient to reason. Thus, people are characterised by a number of 'passions' which, if left in untutored form, lead to negative traits such as foolhardiness, cowardice, lavishness and meanness. So according to Aristotle, people differ according to how successful they are at keeping their 'passions' in check. However, this ability can be acquired. An individual can practise acting in a certain way and thereby alter his/her behaviour. For example, to be generous in temperament rather than mean, a person must actively practise generosity.

A different approach was taken by Galen, a medic around AD 100. As a doctor, Galen was interested in the various glands in the human body and the chemicals they secreted. His theory of personality was based on differences in the individual's physiology. He believed that body chemicals (or **humours**) were mainly responsible for human personality (McConnell, 1974; Gregory, 1987). Four 'humours' were identified by Galen based on his primitive medical knowledge of the time: blood, phlegm, yellow bile and black bile. If individuals were most influenced by their blood, then they were described as sanguine; those influenced by phlegm were said to be phlegmatic; someone influenced by yellow bile was choleric, and someone influenced by black bile was melancholic. These different biochemical constitutions were then assumed to be associated with different personality characteristics. Thus, a sanguine person was supposed to be cheerful, hearty, outgoing, sturdy, fearless, optimistic and interested in physical pleasures; a phlegmatic person was cold, aloof, calm, detached, unemotional, uninvolved, quiet, withdrawn, dependable and dull; a choleric person was easy to rouse to anger, characterised by hate and gave in to bad impulses; a melancholic person was depressed, unhappy and had suicidal tendencies.

These ancient theories seem primitive to the modern personality psychologist. For example, we now know that not all of Galen's humours actually exist, and there is little empirical evidence to link his humours to actual personality types. Nevertheless, theories such as those of Galen and Aristotle represent some of the very first attempts to define the characteristics of people and to differentiate between one person's behaviour and another person's behaviour; they are amongst the first theories of personality and individual differences. Moreover, some of the important issues which concern psychologists today can be traced back to these early beginnings.

Enduring controversies

Importantly, Plato, Aristotle and Galen seem to make different assumptions about personality. To begin with, Plato and Aristotle seem to be saying that differences between individuals are under the individual's control (according to both theorists we can try to become different by practising other behaviours), hence our characters are our responsibility. On the other hand, Galen assumed that our behaviour is determined by our biochemical constitution and is therefore beyond our control. These different assumptions, though seemingly minor at first, increase in importance when we begin to reflect on the implications of each theory for personality change. For Galen, an angry, aggressive individual (choleric) is that way because the yellow bile in his body influences his behaviour. The only way to alter aggression would therefore be to treat the individual by altering his body chemistry. On the other hand, Aristotle assumed that it was possible for an individual to change his behaviour by practising alternative behaviours, hence, it should be sufficient to show people that their behaviour is not acceptable (by punishing bad behaviour, and rewarding good, for example) to induce behavioural change. The implications of these two different assumptions about human nature (whether individuals have control over the way they behave, or not) are still, of course, relevant today. For example, people (psychologists and psychiatrists included) are still divided on whether we should punish criminals to induce them to alter their own behaviour, or whether we should treat them, in much the same way as we might treat a medical condition. These questions relate to what has become known in psychology as the debate over **free will** versus **determinism**. Adherents to the free will position (sometimes called 'Libertarians') assume that people ultimately have control over what they are, whereas determinists assume that our characters are moulded by forces beyond our control.

Another issue illustrated by the writings of Plato, Aristotle and Galen is known as the **mind/body problem**. Plato and Aristotle assumed that reason (mind) could be made to rule passion (an irrational or emotional part of the person). Galen does not mention 'mind' or 'reason' at all in his account; to him, what we are is laid down in our physiological or biochemical constitution. On reflection, both views appear to offer a rather incomplete explanation. Most of us take it for granted that human beings have two 'parts': the part of us that thinks and feels, and the part of us that is matter/physiology. However, we also accept that the brain is part of the body, and that when we think and feel these processes ultimately have a biochemical or physiological basis. When we enquire about what makes a person carry out a particular action, we can think of several reasons, each offering a different level of explanation. The following fictitious conversation illustrates this problem:

'Why did you go out for a walk?'
'I was bored'
'Yes, but why were you bored?'
'There was nothing for me to do'
'Why did you need to do anything?'
'I felt restless with nothing to do'
'How do you know you felt restless?'
'I was fidgeting'
'Why?'
'I don't know! My body was itching to do something!'
'So, why did you decide to go for a walk, rather than do something else?'
'Because I enjoy walking'
'Why do you enjoy walking?'
'Because I have happy memories of going for walks with my mother as a child, and I've liked walking ever since.'

In the above conversation, several reasons are given to justify 'going for a walk': boredom (a state of mind); restlessness (a bodily sensation expressed by fidgeting, a piece of behaviour); and finally a preference is expressed (for walking) which is traced to a childhood experience held in memory (back to mind again!).

Of course, one could argue that all of these states are ultimately biochemically or physiologically derived. This argument assumes that we cannot think, feel or make choices without neural activity from the brain. But, as psychologists who want to understand individual differences in behaviour, we ultimately must still explain why one person's brain leads him/her to do one thing, whilst another individual's leads him/her to behave differently. We could perhaps make Galen's assumption that people are characterised by differences in their biochemical constitutions. Different brains lead to different behaviours. But this presents us with a further problem: ultimately, we would like to be able to explain *how* the brain (a physical entity) translates chemical messages into thoughts and actions which differ from one individual to another. Even if we began with Aristotle's assumption that 'reason' can control 'passion' we are faced with the same problem. How are 'thoughts' and 'experiences' converted into the biochemical and electrochemical messages necessary to act and react? Whichever view you prefer, sooner or later, it will probably occur to you that human behaviour is governed by more than either 'mind' or 'matter' alone. And what about external influences on our behaviour? Consider the following conundrum: 'If your body was sitting in a chair on one side of the room, but your brain was in a bucket at the other side of the room, where would *you* be?' There is no easy answer to this question, but obviously you would be unable to see, feel or hear unless your brain was attached to your body. The person in the fictitious conversation also stated that she enjoyed walking because she walked with her mother as a child. The explanation for this preference is given in terms of past experience, but the experience is still held in memory (mind), which resides in the brain (matter)! There is also a sense in which, without the opportunity to experience via the senses there could be no such thing as 'mind' and therefore no such thing as 'self'. Of course, without a sense of 'self' or 'others' it makes no sense to talk about personality. So for a complete explanation of personality we would need to account for all of the possible interactions between the external world, any biochemical predispositions and something called 'mind' which appears to consist of representations of the world/experience, and matter.

Although our present knowledge of the physiology and biochemistry of the brain has come a long way since the Ancient Greeks and Galen, we have still not solved the mind/body problem. This means that some psychologists have concentrated their efforts on one level of explanation at a time rather than attempting to offer a complete account of all human behaviour, emotion and thought. These different starting points have resulted in some very different approaches to the study of personality and individual differences.

Major psychological influences on personality psychology

As personality psychology is a relatively new area of specialisation within the discipline of psychology in general, it follows that important influences on the study of personality can be traced to various psychological schools of thought, as well as to early philosophers and medics.

Major psychological influences on personality psychology come from: medical approaches to the treatment of mental illness; psycho-physics and psychometrics (psychological measurement); Behaviourism; and **Gestalt psychology** (Hjelle and Ziegler, 1976).

Medical approaches to mental illness

The medical approach to mental illness dealt with the understanding of, classification and treatment of mental disorders. In the early stages, mental dysfunction and the psychology of 'normal' behaviour were distinct disciplines, however the study of mental illness has increasingly influenced the study of 'normal personality'.

Emil Kraepelin (1856–1926) is considered by many to be 'the father of clinical psychology'. His approach to mental dysfunction was that it resulted from organic brain damage, metabolic disorders, endocrinal disturbances or hereditary factors (Eysenck *et al.*, 1975). In other words, like Galen, his theory was based on physiological and biochemical factors although his medical knowledge was, of course, far advanced in comparison. He was one of the first to use a scientific approach to the study of mental disorders, for example, he used objective tests and took systematic measurements. He was also interested in **psychopharmacology**: the study of the effects of drugs on human behaviour. Kraepelin's greatest contribution to personality psychology, however, was manifest through his influence on the work of Ernst Kretschmer in the 1920s.

Kretschmer's view was that there was only a gradual distinction between mental disorders and normality, and he was thus one of the first psychologists to attempt to explain individual differences in terms of differences in psychological adjustment. He proposed a theory of individual differences based on morphology (body type) (Kretschmer, 1925). According to Kretschmer, it is possible to distinguish between three character types or temperaments each associated with a physical build. Each type was assumed to predispose the individual to a different sort of mental disorder. The asthenic type, physically characterised by a narrow trunk, long limbs and a thin face, was described by Kretschmer as introverted, shy, often cold and calculating and rather dull. This type of person has a tendency towards social withdrawal and schizophrenia. The pyknic type has short limbs, a round face, a broad, stocky body and a tendency to gain weight. This type of person according to Kretschmer exhibits wild fluctuations in mood, varying between deep depressions and euphoria and thus tends to manifest the clinical symptoms of manic-depression. Finally, Kretschmer described an athletic type. These individuals have 'balanced' physiques, are muscular, display the personality characteristics of energy and sanguinity and are predisposed towards aggression.

Like Kraepelin, Kretschmer believed that psychopathology had a biochemical basis in hormonal secretions. However, he went further than Kraepelin in his assumption that 'normal'

19

personality can be explained according to the same principles as mental dysfunction (the difference was merely a question of quantity rather than quality). More modern psychoanalytic approaches to personality also make the assumption that individual differences in normal personality have a basis in psychopathology, although they have not retained Kretschmer's assumption that individual differences are associated with physical types.

Another early theory of personality types based on morphology was that of W.H. Sheldon. Working in the early 1940s and 1950s, Sheldon's descriptions were similar to those of Kretschmer. However, Sheldon's theory was based on 'normal' people rather than on the personality and physical characteristics of mental patients. Sheldon (1942) and Sheldon *et al.* (1940) took detailed measurements of male college students and drew conclusions regarding the link between physical type and personality characteristics. Sheldon described three physical types: endo-morphs (who have soft, rounded bodies and large stomachs), meso-morphs (who have hard, square, muscular bodies) and ecto-morphs (tall and thin with large heads). According to Sheldon, whereas endomorphs are sociable individuals, meso-morphs are athletic, competitive, courageous and sanguine and ecto-morphs are inhibited, introverted and intellectual. He also believed that the physical and personality make-up of all individuals is genetically determined. Your physical shape and personality characteristics are both assumed by Sheldon to be linked to a genetic blueprint inherited from your parents.

The three theories described illustrate the progressive influence of clinical medicine on the study of personality and individual differences. Although the concept of individual differences in personality based on body morphology is no longer widely accepted today, the main legacy of medical approaches to mental illness is in the view that individual differences in the characteristic patterns of behaviour we exhibit have a physiological, biochemical or genetic basis, and that behaviours which are psychopathological differ from 'normal' non-pathological behaviour only in the extent to which we differ from each other in terms of our underlying physiology. This view is still apparent today in psychoanalytic approaches to personality and in modern psychiatry. The key to understanding mental illness, criminal behaviour, aggression, or what makes one person sociable and another reserved is, therefore, to be found in their underlying physiological constitutions. It follows from this view that the use of drugs to alter our biochemistry will also result in changes to our personality and behaviour. Thus, modern day psychiatrists use drugs in combination with other forms of therapy in the treatment of psychopathology.

Psycho-physics and psychometrics

Psychometrics is the science of psychological measurement. Before the advent of psychometrics it was not possible to measure aspects of human psychological functioning because so much of what we experience is implicit (unobservable) and therefore unverifiable. Psychology was not therefore a science by modern standards because it relied on introspection (subject's self-reports of their feelings and experiences). **Psychometric methods** helped to make psychology accepted as a truly scientific discipline.

The basic psychometric methodology can be traced to the work in psycho-physics of Ernst Heinrich Weber (1795–1878), a professor of anatomy and physiology (Eysenck *et al.*, 1975). Weber was investigating the sense of touch. He tried to establish the least difference that could be distinguished between two points of stimulation on the skin (for example, when two needles are lightly placed on the back of the hand, a blindfolded person will report that he/she can feel two points of sensation, however when the needles are placed closer and closer together, there comes a time when only one point is detected). He concluded from his research that very slight differences between stimuli are experienced as equivalent and suggested that this is because when nerve fibres in close proximity are stimulated, a single neuronal message is perceived. He also noted that the intensity of the stimulus (needle pressure) and size has an effect on the ability to distinguish between two stimuli. He found that these basic rules seemed to apply to all sorts of sensations. For example, there is a **threshold** at which we can first distinguish a point of light at which it is just bright enough or large enough for us to see it.

Weber's observations were later followed up by Gustav Fechner (1801–1887). Fechner, a physicist and philosopher, was one of the first people to propose that there might be an observable and therefore measurable relationship between the external world and our internal response to it (Eysenck *et al.*, 1975). Thus, Weber and Fechner carried out research which made possible a quantifiable relationship between the physical and mental spheres.

The influence of Weber and Fechner on modern psychometric testing can be traced to the basic idea that we can infer something about the implicit (unobservable) psychological characteristics of people, like attitudes and dispositions, and measure differences between people on these characteristics. This reasoning is apparent today in modern psychometric tests of personality. Psychometric methods really came to fruition with the advent of statistical techniques. For instance, in 1904 Spearman developed a methodology called factor analysis based on statistics to measure intelligence and thus set the scene for the statistical measurement of personality traits. We will examine Spearman's contribution more closely in Chapter 4.

Behaviourism

The behaviourist school was influenced by the philosophical tradition of **dualism** expounded by René Descartes (1596–1650) (Eysenck *et al.*, 1975). Descartes emphasised the distinction between 'mind' and 'body' as radically distinct and incompatible substances which nevertheless interact. For Descartes, although the body (matter) occupied space and could be known by science, the mind was incorporeal and mysterious. Whilst he acknowledged that mind and body interact (when you knock your elbow, you feel pain) he never unravelled the nature of this interaction (he was one of the first people to define the mind/body problem as an issue).

The behaviourists, working much later in the late 1800s and early 1900s, re-examined some of the issues acknowledged by

Descartes and came to the conclusion that in order to maintain a truly scientific orientation towards the study of human behaviour, it was necessary to reject the concept of mind. As 'mind' is impossible to measure, it was considered to be irrelevant. Instead, the behaviourists focused on 'behaviour', which *is* observable. They therefore laid the foundations for what was to become an objective, scientific study of behaviour. J.B. Watson (1878–1958) was one of the earliest behaviourists. He was interested in how changes in behaviour could be brought about by learned associations between events. One of his earliest experiments involved presenting a young child (often referred to as 'little Albert') with a white rat (Watson and Raynor, 1920). At first Albert's reaction to the rat was inquisitive and trusting. However, when the rat was then presented accompanied by a loud noise, the child began to cry and show a fear response. Eventually, after several pairings of the rat and the loud noise, the young child reacted to the rat with fear and his previous trusting behaviour had disappeared.

Watson's observations were later extended by Hull, Tolman and eventually Skinner, whose experiments are described in Chapter 3. As a behaviourist, Watson rejected subjective experiences as a suitable subject of study for psychologists and modern personality theories influenced by the behaviourist school have therefore tended to emphasise learning experiences throughout life, rather than underlying physiological or psychological characteristics. In this respect, they can be contrasted with psychoanalytic approaches to personality because they reject medical models of normal and abnormal behaviour. Thus, a fearful person is seen as someone who has learned to associate many situations with negative experiences (just as Albert learned to associate the rat with an unpleasant loud noise) rather than someone who has a 'nervous disposition'. The tendency of the behaviourists to reject 'mind' however has led to the criticism that they have ignored an important aspect of human nature: thought processes. Modern theories of personality based on learning have therefore tended to adopt a less extreme position; for instance, whereas modern social-learning theories accept the view that personality is essentially the sum total of a person's learning experiences from birth onwards, thought processes nevertheless have a major part to play in their theoretical model.

Also, as according to the behaviourist position, individual differences can best be explained in terms of different learning environments (nurture or upbringing) rather than in terms of physiology, biochemistry or genetics (nature, or innate predispositions), they can further be contrasted with any theory of personality which assumes that we inherit our personality from our parents. The distinction between nature and nurture has proved particularly controversial in the field of personality and individual differences and is referred to often as the nature versus nurture debate. Although few psychologists today rigidly adhere to one or the other position, theorists still differ considerably in the extent to which they emphasise the role of genetics and upbringing in accounting for individual differences.

Gestalt psychology

The term 'Gestalt' in German approximates in meaning to the English 'form', 'figure', 'configuration' or 'structure'. The Gestalt school of psychology was founded in 1912 by Max Wertheimer (see Beardslee and Wertheimer (1958) for a translation of his work). Wertheimer's original interest was in the field of perception and perceptual processes. The Gestalt psychologists emphasised 'complexity' rather than 'simple stimuli' and their focus of study was the 'holistic' nature of perception. Wertheimer argued that there are relationships in which all that occurs in the whole is not dependent on the nature and combination of the individual parts (Beardslee and Wertheimer, 1958). To understand what Wertheimer meant, consider a human facial expression. We understand the overall expression as one which denotes 'happiness' or 'sadness' but if we were asked to define exactly what it is about the individual features which lead us to understand the person's mood, we would find this difficult to explain. According to the Gestalt view, the principles we use to group objects in the external world come from our perceptual

system (including the brain), and what we see does not necessarily correspond to what actually exists 'out there'. Perception
is therefore more than the sum of points of light hitting the retina.
We impose a structure on what we perceive. This structure comes
from within, not without, and the basic rules we use to group
incoming stimuli together or detect sensations as separate are
assumed to be innate or inherited.

The influence of the Gestalt view that 'the whole is greater
than the sum of parts' can best be seen in those personality theories which emphasise 'the whole person' in contrast with those
which attempt to break down human personality into components for study. Gestalt psychology has thus had a major influence
on modern phenomenological or humanist theories (see Chapter
3). Gestalt psychology has also had an important influence on
some theories of social perception (see Chapter 6). Theories influenced by Gestalt psychology can be contrasted with learning
approaches based on behaviourist principles because they assume
that we should look within the person to understand what we
are, whereas behaviourists have tended to look outside the person,
to cues in situations which trigger behaviour. They can be further
contrasted with trait or psychometric approaches, because the
psychometric view that we can measure differences between
aspects of psychological functioning conflicts with the Gestalt view
that 'the whole is greater than the sum of parts'.

Personality psychology today

In this chapter it has been suggested that the influences on personality psychology can be traced to various schools of thought which
are often contradictory. One important area of disagreement
between theorists concerns the issue of subjectivity versus objec-
tivity. That is, whether the assumptions they make about human
psychological functioning are empirically testable. For instance,
we saw that whilst some approaches have focused on dynamics
within the person (medical approaches and Gestalt approaches
for instance), the behaviourists rejected implicit, unobservable

characteristics as unscientific, choosing to focus instead on explicit behaviour. On the other hand, it was suggested that the study of implicit human psychological functioning need not be considered unscientific, provided that implicit constructs could be measured in a scientific way, and that this became possible with the advent of psychometrics: the science of psychological measurement.

A second area of disagreement concerns different views over which aspects of human nature psychologists should be concerned with. It was noted that Gestalt psychology rejects an elemental-istic approach to the study of human nature because according to the Gestalt view human psychological functioning can only be understood as a whole. This view is thus incompatible with the psychometric approach which focuses on the measurement of specific aspects of psychological functioning. Furthermore, the behaviourist emphasis on observable behaviour has been criticised for ignoring physiology and thought processes as important areas of study.

Each of these schools or approaches within psychology represents a different starting point in the study of the person and each is associated with its own peculiar methods, assumptions and subject samples. Consequently, personality psychology has also developed according to different schools or approaches. The main approaches to personality psychology are dealt with in Chapters 3 and 4.

Summary

The study of personality psychology represents an amalgam of influences from 'amateur philosophers' or lay personality theorists, to the academic disciplines of philosophy, anatomy, physiology, biochemistry, psycho-physics and statistics. Each of these fields has contributed specific methodologies and approaches to studying the person, many of which have undergone considerable modifi-cation and development over time. Despite the inevitable advances in scientific thought and methodology, however, many of the issues which concern students of personality and individual differences today have endured. These include the issue of free-will versus determinism; the mind/body problem; and the nature/nurture debate.

Further reading

Hjelle, L.A. and Ziegler, D.J. (1976). *Personality: Basic Assumptions, Research and Applications*. McGraw-Hill. Chapter 1: The nature of personality. A very good introduction to the philosophical issues which have concerned students of human behaviour and personality for centuries.

Gardner, H., Kornhaber, M.L. and Wake, W.K. (1996). *Intelligence: Multiple Perspectives*. Harcourt Brace. Chapter 2: Origins of the scientific perspective. Although this text focuses on intelligence, Chapter 2 is relevant to the study of personality and individual differences in general.

Chapter 3

Personality
and
individuality

29

IN CHAPTER 2 IT WAS SUGGESTED THAT personality psychologists differ according to whether they prefer to focus on human psychological functioning, human behaviour, physiology, or a mixture of these, in their theories. Nevertheless, it is possible to distinguish between a number of broad types of approach or perspective and the following classifications are the same as those found in most major personality textbooks: the psychoanalytic perspective (whose main influence can be traced to clinical medicine), the social-learning approach (influenced by the behaviourist school), the phenomenological approach (influenced by Gestalt psychology); and the trait approach (based on psychometric methods). However, many textbooks make a further distinction between 'ideographic' approaches and 'nomothetic' approaches. Ideographic approaches focus on how basic laws of human nature (biological instincts, laws of learning, motivation) can give rise to uniqueness amongst individuals, whereas nomothetic approaches attempt to identify personality dimensions which can be quantified or measured and used to compare groups of individuals. Both these approaches assume that people's behaviour, thoughts and perceptions are mediated by underlying personality dispositions or temperaments. However, according to the ideographic approach, comparing one group of people to another group of people along a dispositional dimension such as sociability or anxiety cannot ever give a full picture of personality because personality is 'idiosyncratic' and each individual has his/her own unique temperament. The aim of ideographic personality theories is, therefore, to explain human individuality rather than to quantify personality differences between groups of individuals. Examples of ideographic approaches are psychoanalytic approaches, social-learning approaches and phenomenological (or humanist) approaches which will be dealt with in this chapter. The trait approach to personality which has tended to adopt a nomothetic methodology will be introduced later, in Chapter 4.

The psychoanalytic approach to personality

The psychoanalytic approach to personality arose from the clinical observations of Sigmund Freud (1856–1939), whose work has influenced psychoanalytic theorists throughout this century. Freud's observations were based on clinical patients (mainly female) who were referred to him with symptoms of neurosis. The psychoanalytic approach was then applied to an understanding of personality in general, initially by Freud himself (Freud, 1953), but later on by post-Freudian psychoanalytic theorists. As psycho-analytic psychology has mainly concerned itself with the understanding of clinical cases, psychoanalytic approaches have emphasised personality dysfunction. This has led many psycholo-gists to criticise Freud for painting a negative view of human nature (for example, Erikson, 1963), and since then his basic ideas have undergone considerable modification. Despite modifications to the original theory, however, all psychoanalytic psychologists make similar basic assumptions about the development of personality: they assume that personality and individuality arise from conflicts experienced at stages in human development and that the various ways in which conflicts are resolved depend primarily on the early childhood environment. Thus, whereas the basic conflicts encoun-tered are the same for all, it is our experiences in resolving these conflicts that ultimately make us unique. Furthermore, whether we are destined to become essentially psychologically healthy or psychologically unhealthy depends on our relative success in over-coming conflict throughout development.

Freud's psychoanalytic theory

Freud's theory encompasses many areas of human psychological function and dysfunction, so the following sections will only describe the aspects of his theory which are relevant to the development of personality (Freud, 1953; 1962; 1933). According to Freud, a major source of psychological conflict is a biological battle between instincts, mainly sexual (life instincts or **eros**) and aggressive (death instincts or **thanatos**), and the demands imposed by our environment as to whether it is socially acceptable to express these instincts. Freud saw human beings in terms of energy systems, in which sexual and aggressive energies build up until they are able to find an appropriate release. In the absence of a vehicle for release, the individual is in an unhealthy state of tension. Initially, the infant has no option but to express its instincts in an uninhibited way via reflex actions such as defecation or suckling. The infant is impulsive, irrational and narcissistic (self-loving) and responds only to achieve instant gratification for its urges, regardless of whether this is appropriate, or harmful, and its behaviour though self-gratifying, consequently often brings displeasure to its parents. At this stage the infant is said to be dominated by the id, a hypothetical structure which is unconscious and unavailable to awareness.

Mechanisms for tension reduction become progressively more useful throughout development as the infant learns to **delay gratification**. Gradually, the infant learns that in order to please its parents it must only seek gratification for its instincts when this is socially acceptable. Two events in the child's early life which are important in this process are weaning and toilet training. The child must learn not to expect milk whenever it is hungry or to defecate at will, but that it must wait until the time and place are appropriate. The **ego**, a second hypothetical structure, thus forms in interaction with the environment as the infant learns to inhibit its instinctual tendencies according to social demands. However, the basic instincts which dominated the *id* still motivate behaviour, and the child must learn to tolerate moderate tension through the use of **ego defence mechanisms** which inhibit, gradually release energy or divert it into appropriate activities. Thus, once the child has an ego it can deal with its instincts in an 'intellectual' not 'emotional' way. Nevertheless, the defence mechanisms are not always successful, and unconscious emotions and instincts which have been inhibited may manifest themselves in psychosomatic illness and neuroses.

The final hypothetical structure to be achieved according to Freud is the **superego**. This last structure is acquired via socialisation. Although the child dominated by its ego is able to delay gratification, the main motivation for this is parental pleasure or displeasure. In the absence of its parents, the motivation for delaying gratification is no longer present. At some point, the child must come to internalise society's standards and to know 'right' from 'wrong'. This is achieved via two superego subsystems: the conscience and the ego-ideal. The mechanism by which the conscience controls behaviour is guilt. This emotion occurs when the individual transgresses, even in the absence of parents, and motivates the adult to behave 'properly' in order to avoid guilty feelings. The ego-ideal operates by rewarding the individual in the absence of parental rewards for good behaviour and provides the basis for internalised self-esteem. With the development of a superego self-control replaces parental control. By this stage, the adult can tolerate considerable tension arising from the ever-present underlying instincts, because it has an ever more sophisticated array of ego defence mechanisms to assist it. Amongst the array of defence mechanisms available proposed by Freud are **repression** (whereby unacceptable thoughts are pushed out of awareness); **sublimation** (whereby sexual/aggressive energy can be diverted into healthy activities such as painting or sport); **projection** (as in prejudiced attitudes, in which one's own unacceptable impulses are projected onto others); **displacement** (whereby impulses are redirected onto a less threatening person, such as taking out aggression towards your boss on your family); **rationalisation** (distorting reality to bolster your own self-esteem); **reaction formation** (expressing attitudes which conflict with your emotions, such as going on a crusade against sexual promiscuity to disguise your own sexual feelings) and **denial** (refusing to accept the truth). (See Freud, A., 1966.)

Freud and personality

According to Freud the whole of adult life represents a series of conflicts between the demands of the instincts of the *id* and the demands of society represented by the ego (external demands) and superego (internalised demands). Individuals differ according to how successfully they can achieve a balance between these structures. One source of individual variation can therefore be the extent to which a particular person makes use of the various ego defence mechanisms proposed by Freud. Hence a number of personality psychologists have investigated individual differences in the use of specific Freudian defence mechanisms (for example, an individual difference in the tendency to repress emotions is suggested by Byrne, 1961). However, the mechanism which Freud himself thought mainly responsible for individual differences in personality was 'fixation', 'whereby vestiges of behaviour left over from early stages in development are carried over into adult life. If a person is dominated by the more primitive structures, then he/she will exhibit dysfunctional characteristics. For example, an individual who is dominated by the demands of the *id* will be predominantly impulsive, selfish and narcissistic and without the control of the ego and superego will only act to achieve self-gratification, regardless of the consequences to others. Similarly, someone who has an ego but no superego will have no conscience and may well behave unsociably as long as there is little risk of being found out. The basic idea that people can become fixated at stages in their development has had an important influence on many post-Freudian psychoanalytic theories of criminality, sexual deviancy and aggression (Hollin, 1989).

Freud himself proposed that fixation could occur at very specific stages in psycho-sexual development, each associated with personality characteristics in adulthood. Thus Freud described an **oral personality**, whose characteristics derive from an oral stage in development, in which sexual and aggressive energy is centred around the region of the mouth and suckling behaviour. At this first developmental stage, the *id*-dominated infant must undergo the trauma of having its demands for milk rejected by its mother in the process of weaning. If the mother is too indulgent (allows the infant to breast feed for too long) or frustrates the child (by being overly rejecting or inconsistent) the infant will be fixated at the oral stage and will be either over-trusting and dependent in adulthood (oral passive personality) or, alternatively, characterised by cynicism, dominance and exploitativeness (oral sadistic personality). The next of Freud's psycho-sexual stages is the **anal stage**, in which sexual energy is centred around the anal region and the conflict for the child is associated with toilet training activity. Again, parental over-indulgence or frustration produce anal personality types characterised by the traits of obstinacy, orderliness, punctuality, or cruelty, destructiveness, hostility and possessiveness in adult relationships. Finally, Freud proposed an **Oedipal personality** type, whose characteristics derive from the phallic stage of development during which sexual energy is centred around the genital area. According to Freud all children at this stage sexually desire the parent of the opposite sex. Thus males will desire their mothers and females their fathers. How parents react to their child's awakening sexuality at this stage will influence whether the child becomes fixated at the phallic stage and thus exhibit the following characteristics: the child will be brash, vain, boastful and ambitious (if male) and flirtatious, seductive and promiscuous (if female).

Empirical verification of Freud's theory

One of the main problems with Freud's theory of personality is that it is based on evidence derived from the psychoanalytic methodology which was devised mainly for use in a clinical context. In **psychoanalysis**, the clients are usually patients presenting with various symptoms of neurosis which Freud believed represented the manifestation of repressed experiences and emotions which have been pushed out of awareness. The aim of psychoanalysis is therefore to 'release' repressed feelings into awareness so that individuals can deal with them in a healthier more effective way and thus free themselves of the neurosis. Many proponents of Freud argue that the effectiveness of psychoanalysis is itself evidence in support of Freud's model (Kline, 1984). However, others have argued that psychoanalysis is not always effective, and that even if it were, psychoanalysis as a treatment for neurosis does not provide evidence for Freud's ideas as they apply to normal personality development (Stevens, 1983). Furthermore, attempts to test Freud's psycho-sexual theory of personality using modern experimental psychological methods have been somewhat inconclusive (Eysenck, 1986). Despite disputes over the empirical validity of Freud's clinical observations as they relate to personality, some argue that this should not cause us to reject the theory outright (Kline, 1984). Instead, we should acknowledge that we simply have not developed a methodology which is sensitive enough to test Freud's ideas at present.

In addition to the general empirical criticisms, a number of specific criticisms have also been levelled at Freud. One prevailing view is that Freud's theory is too deterministic. According to Freud, personality is shaped very early on in childhood and there is little room for people to alter their basic personality characteristics throughout life. Freud did not accept that individuals have 'free will'. Also, his emphasis on sex and aggression as the main motivators of human behaviour neglects the many social facets of human behaviour and seems to offer a pessimistic account of human personality (Hjelle and Ziegler, 1981a).

Erikson's psycho-social psychoanalytic theory

An alternative psychoanalytic model of human personality development is that of Erik Erikson (1963). Erikson's theory answers some of the criticisms levelled at Freud by suggesting that human personality development is motivated by maturational steps within a social environment from birth until death. Erikson retained the concept of stages present in Freud's account of personality development, but extended these to cover the lifespan. The theory is based on the psychoanalytic idea that personality develops through conflict resolutions. However, the conflicts to be resolved are social conflicts, according to Erikson, and not sexual conflicts.

Erikson based his theory on what he termed his 'epigenetic' principle. Personality develops according to genetically predetermined maturational steps but the sequence and rate of psychological growth depends on social opportunity. For example, learning to talk and sexual maturity are genetically predetermined to occur at specific maturational stages in human development. However, for the child to develop psychologically, adequate social opportunities must exist for it to practice social skills and meet sexual partners. According to Erikson, society is structured so as to provide such opportunities. For example, formal schooling is timed to begin when children have acquired enough language to communicate with their peers and social functions such as parties/discos are encouraged in teenagehood so that young people can meet with potential sexual partners. Each stage presents a new conflict which individuals must overcome successfully in order to function as psychologically healthy individuals. The most well-known of these conflicts occurs in adolescence when young people experience an **identity crisis** which, if resolved successfully results in a sense of self but if unresolved results in role confusion. Erikson proposed eight stages associated with conflicting social roles (shown here in brackets): the oral-sensory stage in the first year of life (trust versus mistrust); the muscular-anal stage in the second year (autonomy versus shame); the locomotor-genital stage between three and five years of age (initiative versus guilt); the latency stage from 6 until puberty (industry versus inferiority); adolescence (identity versus role confusion); early adulthood (intimacy versus isolation); middle adulthood (generativity versus self-absorption) and mature adulthood (integrity versus despair).

Erikson and personality

According to Erikson, personality is seen as the extent to which a person is characterised by the positive or negative elements at each stage. For example, you could be a mistrustful person, who is industrious, yet fears intimacy resulting in social isolation, or a trusting, intimate individual who experiences role conflict, and so on. One advantage of Erikson's theory over that of Freud is that changing conditions are assumed to override previous stages in personality development, so that somebody who emerges from the oral-sensory stage as mistrustful can regain their trust at a later stage, if given the right environment. For instance, a young adult may learn to trust people despite an insecure childhood. Another advantage is that the theory is more amenable to empirical verification and a few studies have provided evidence to support some of Erikson's psycho-social constructs (Hjelle and Ziegler, 1981b).

The social-learning approach

The **social-learning** perspective on personality is based on the behaviourist philosophy that all behaviour is initiated and maintained by our experiences after birth. Thus, the human infant at birth is likened to a '*tabula rasa*' or 'blank slate' and everything that we become has been learned within our own individual learning environment.

Background to social-learning theory

The social learning view represents a development of the observations of Pavlov (1927) and Skinner (1938) in relation to learning in animals.

Pavlov, a Russian physiologist, based his original experiment around the natural tendency for a dog to salivate in the presence of food. He noticed that a dog could learn a simple association between the presence of a tone and the presentation of food. If the tone immediately preceded food over a number of trials, the dog would eventually salivate to the tone even when it was not followed by food. Pavlov concluded that the animal had learned to associate the tone with feeding. He called this form of associative learning **classical conditioning** (Pavlov, 1927).

The simple associations demonstrated in classical conditioning, however, are based on situations in which the animal is passive. The animal relies on the experimenter to present the cues (a tone, food) and does not have an active role in the learning situation. Later studies have shown that associative learning can also apply to contexts in which the animal is a more active participant in the learning situation (Skinner, 1938). These studies demonstrate that an animal can also form an association between a behavioural response initiated by itself, and the consequences of its behaviour. If its behaviour has positive consequences, the behaviour will be **reinforced** and thus repeated again in future. On the other hand, if the consequences are negative, the behaviour will be avoided (**punishment**). For example, a cat will soon learn to scratch at the back door if this has the consequence of being let in to be fed or sit by the fire. However, if its owner reacts to having her door scratched by spraying the cat with a jet of water, the cat will soon stop destroying the paintwork! This type of association between a behaviour initiated by the animal and its consequences is known as **operant conditioning**. The basic principles of operant conditioning were developed and extended by Skinner, whose experiments identified a number of rules of operant conditioning which govern the maintenance of animal behaviour. Based on these studies, he coined the terms **extinction**, to describe the gradual decline of responding when reinforcement has been withheld for several trials; **generalisation**, to describe when a learned response to one stimulus is generalised to other similar stimuli (e.g. when a conditioned response to a high pitched tone is displayed also to low pitched tones); **discrimination learning**, the opposite of generalisation, to describe when the animal is conditioned to respond only to highly specific stimuli (e.g. a tone of a particular pitch only when it is presented in the presence of a light); and **reinforcement schedule** to describe the sequence in which the animal is reinforced (for instance the animal may be reinforced after every response or every ten responses, after several seconds or several minutes, and so on).

Skinner did not attempt to account for his observations in terms of an underlying theory. As a behaviourist, he believed that psychologists should not make subjective speculations about the causes of behaviour based on unobservable events such as 'thought' or little understood physiological principles. Instead, they should only be concerned with **behavioural prediction** (using the rules of conditioning to predict future behaviour). He further believed that any behaviour in animals and humans could be

shaped according to the principles of operant conditioning and that even very complex behaviours represent nothing other than chains of responses which have been reinforced at each stage (Skinner, 1971). One example of an applied clinical use of **shaping** is thus to teach basic self-care skills to learning disabled people. For instance, to teach the person to feed him/herself, behaviours such as holding the spoon, bringing it close to their mouth, can be reinforced in stages by rewarding the person with something he/she cherishes (praise, treats) and behaviours which are inappropriate can be ignored or extinguished.

Conditioning and behaviour

The principles of operant conditioning outlined by Skinner have had important implications for personality theorists, because they imply that there is no need to assume a basis for people's behaviour in temperaments or personality dispositions. If we accept the extreme position of behaviourists like Skinner, we could theoretically account for everything that we are in terms of the situations which we have encountered from birth onwards, and the unique pattern of reinforcements and punishments associated with those situations. However, operant conditioning assumes that before a behaviour can be maintained by reinforcement, we must first carry out that behaviour (or an approximation to it) by trial and error so that we can experience its consequences and thus learn to associate the consequence with our own actions. Behaviour which arises 'accidentally' through trial and error cannot be attributed to dispositional differences between people, because it occurs at random. Moreover, if each of us had to experience an accident in order to learn to avoid walking in front of traffic, few of us would survive the ordeal! In reality, we do not necessarily have to perform a response to learn. Indeed, there are many things which we know how to do by observing other people, which we have never actually done. Skinner's principles have therefore needed some modification in order to offer a complete account of human learning and human personality in all its complexity.

Social-learning theories

Like Skinner, social-learning theorists such as Bandura (1977) assume that reinforcement and punishment maintain behaviour. However, whereas according to Skinner we simply react to external reinforcers by repeating those behaviours which have accidentally been reinforced in the past, for Bandura, we actively seek out situations which will lead to reinforcement and actively avoid situations which will lead to punishment. We are able to do this because we have our own individual expectancies about which situations are most likely to lead to reinforcement and which situations are most likely to lead to punishment. As expectancies can determine how people behave, social learning theories assume that characteristics of the person have a role to play in determining behaviour over and above that of external reinforcers. To the extent that people may be characterised by collections of expectancies which define them uniquely and which affect how they are likely to behave in many different situations, social learning theories of behaviour are therefore also personality theories.

According to Bandura, we will pay particular attention to whether others have been reinforced or punished for their behaviour because this will allow us to anticipate when we ourselves are likely to be reinforced or punished. We therefore acquire expectancies about the consequences of various behaviours through observational learning. If we observe that someone's behaviour leads to pleasant consequences in a particular context, this will encourage us to try that behaviour ourselves in the same context because we anticipate feeling pleasant. Rewards and punishments are therefore experienced internally as pleasant/unpleasant emotional reactions to social situations. People are thus seen as being motivated by implicit rewards and punishments, rather than as automatons, whose behaviour is under the control of external reinforcers. Some aspects of personality are therefore seen as **implicit** rather than **explicit** and this represents a departure from the behaviourist tradition of 'thought' or 'cognition' as irrelevant to the study of behaviour.

According to Bandura, learning takes two basic forms: **obser-vational learning** (our internal emotional reactions to the rewards and punishments of other people) and **modelling** (whereby we imitate behaviours we have previously seen to be rewarded in others). In observational learning, we need not produce a learned response, we merely learn the likely outcome of displaying a particular piece of behaviour, whereas in modelling we reproduce the behaviour ourselves. Whether we actually reproduce a piece of behaviour depends on our perceived ability to reproduce it and our cognitive appraisal of the situation (our expectancies). For example, we may learn a dance by observation, but we may not actually attempt to reproduce the dance steps (the learned behaviour will be **inhibited**). Whether we choose to display the learned behaviour (**disinhibition**) will depend on whether we perceive we have the necessary skills to carry it off in a way which will lead to reward, rather than ridicule! Of course, if we do attempt to imitate the dance steps, thereafter we will be moti-vated to learn the whole sequence if we are reinforced for our efforts rather than punished or (perhaps more embarrassing) ignored! However, we need not depend on the presence of other people to reinforce our behaviour, we may maintain our own behaviour by monitoring our own performance and evaluating it. If the effect is self-reinforcing we will repeat a behavioural sequence and if it is displeasing we will correct the response until we feel it is satisfying.

Social-learning and personality

According to Bandura then, people's internal or implicit expectan-cies of reward and punishment are major determinants of their behaviour and these expectancies are acquired via observa-tional learning and modelling. Individual differences in behaviour therefore arise because different people have been exposed to different sorts of models, and thus people are characterised by their own unique set of expectations of reinforcement and punishment. This goes beyond the Skinnerian view that differ-ences in behaviour only occur because of the actual ways in which we are reinforced or punished within specific situations. Social learning can therefore account for differences in behaviour in terms of the different characteristics of people, over and above the cues present in situations which reinforce or punish our responses.

There is much evidence for the social-learning view that behaviour can be modelled from all sorts of social contexts (Bandura *et al.*, 1961; Bandura and Walters, 1963). However, although most psychologists accept the concept of modelling in principle, in practice it is not always easy to establish exactly what it is about an individual's environment which has led to his or her individual expectations of reinforcement and punishment. For example, it is one thing to argue that an aggressive person has come from an environment in which aggression is frequently seen to be rewarded and infrequently punished, but quite another to establish exactly how it is that an aggressive person's environment is different from that of someone with a similar upbringing who does not expect to be rewarded for aggression and who consequently does not behave aggressively. Of course, no two people have experienced exactly the same social environment, but although this is undoubtedly true, if we cannot identify precisely what it is that initiates and maintains aggressive behaviour, we cannot easily implement a strategy for modifying the behaviour and thus demonstrate the underlying causes empirically. This problem has meant that social-learning theories which rely solely on observational learning and modelling as an explanation for individual differences in personality have been open to criticism from psychologists who argue that inherited characteristics may be equally important determinants of our expectancies and therefore of our behaviour. Consequently, many theorists have used the basic principles of learning in association with inherited predispositions to explain personality. An example is Hans Eysenck (see Chapter 4), whose theory of extraversion is based on the view that extroverts have inherited a physiological predisposition which makes them difficult to condition, whereas the physiology of introverts makes them easily conditionable.

Humanistic theories and the phenomenological perspective on personality

The psychoanalytic approach and the social-learning view of personality both assume that prior determinants affect a person's present behaviour. These prior determinants are the resolution of conflicts throughout development for the psychoanalytic theorist, and past experience of behaviours seen to be rewarded or punished for the social-learning theorist. Both of these approaches are relatively deterministic because they assume that past events outside the individual's control shape present personality (we cannot be held responsible for our failures to resolve conflicts or for the models we have been exposed to) and therefore people do not have complete free will. Phenomenological approaches reject this deterministic view of the person. They prefer to focus on the individual's interpretation of ongoing events and thus see behaviour as determined by the choices we make at a given moment in time. Phenomenologists view the person as an active force pursuing further goals and striving to realise his/her potential and this autonomy means that the individual has more free will. Also, as humanist theorists are interested in people's here and now interpretations of themselves, they emphasise the 'whole' person and reject a reductionist approach which breaks down human nature into components for study.

Maslow's phenomenological theory

One influential phenomenological theory is that of Abraham Maslow. According to Maslow (1970), all human beings have basic important needs: physiological needs (eating, sleeping); safety needs (shelter); belongingness/love needs (relationships/ friendships); **self-esteem** needs (valuing yourself) and **self-actualisation** (realising your full potential). He saw these needs in terms of a hierarchy so that previous needs must be satisfied before later needs can be met. Thus, to achieve self-actualisation we must have food, shelter, love and a sense of self-worth. For Maslow, all individuals are capable of self-actualisation, and although people can vary according to how self-actualised they are at a given stage in their lives, we all have the capability to become self-actualised. The self-actualised person is described by Maslow as someone who has achieved an efficient perception of reality, acceptance of self and others, is spontaneous, creative, has a sense of humour, is democratic (i.e. free of prejudice), autonomous (independent) and has 'peak experiences' (the ability to feel great happiness). However, Maslow did not conceive of the self-actualised person as having a particular character, instead, self-actualisation is more a philosophy of life achievable by everybody. Neither did he assume that a person who is not self-actualised is 'dysfunctional' or psychologically 'unhealthy'. In fact, he emphasised the need to study those aspects of human nature which represent psychological health rather than dysfunction and was critical of what he termed the 'crippled psychology' of the psychoanalytic perspective.

Carl Rogers' phenomenological theory

Whereas Maslow rejected a clinical approach to the study of human behaviour, Rogers' theory is very much concerned with psychological breakdown. According to Rogers (1959), individuals have two ways of interpreting themselves: the self-concept (what we perceive we are) and the ideal self (what we would like to be). Individuals constantly strive to achieve their ideal selves and compare what they feel they are like (self-concept) with what they would like to become (ideal self). Therefore, like Maslow, Rogers saw individuals as striving towards perfectionist goals. However, whereas for Maslow only a failure to satisfy early needs in the hierarchy can interfere with self-actualisation, for Rogers the self-concept can conflict with reality resulting in anxiety. For example, if you think that you are loved, attractive and intelligent but you are rejected by your parents, you cannot get a date or you fail your exams, you will experience a conflict between your self-concept and external reality. Of course, as things do not often work out in accordance with our self-concepts, we must have a mechanism in place to bolster our self-esteem.

According to Rogers, most of the time we can use defences such as perceptual distortion (altering our perception of the world to fit our self-concept, such as deciding that the exam we failed was unfair) to maintain a sense of worth. However, when the defences are not effective we will experience psychological breakdown.

Rogers, unlike Maslow, also attempted to account for the development of a healthy sense of self. According to Rogers, children are born without a sense of self and their feelings of self-worth are governed only by the need to be loved and highly regarded by others. Rogers called this the **organismic valuing process**. As parental love is often conditional (parents often praise their children for doing things which please them rather than for expressing their individuality), children initially sacrifice their own needs in order to gain parental love. However, we all need **unconditional positive regard** in order to become fully functioning people. The absence of unconditional love or unconditional positive regard hampers growth towards self-enhancement and is another underlying cause of psychological ill-health. Rogers outlined the characteristics of the fully-functioning person in the following terms: he/she can experience feelings without threat, is flexible, adaptive, tolerant and spontaneous. The person trusts their feelings and is not guided by group norms, is creative and shows experiential freedom. Thus, an individual who has not been given unconditional positive regard will be more likely to feel threatened by his or her emotions, inflexible, conform to group norms and so on. In order to change, all that is required is an environment in which the person is valued unconditionally, such as in **client-centred therapy**. Here, the person can regain a sense of self-acceptance and thus continue to grow towards self-fulfilment and self-enhancement.

For Rogers, therefore, people have less free will than Maslow implied. Nevertheless, as both Maslow and Rogers assume that human beings strive to achieve ideals of behaviour, this means that people can exercise a degree of choice in relation to what they aspire to. This element of choice differentiates the phenomenological approach to human individuality from that of Bandura or the psychoanalytic theorists because psychoanalytic approaches imply that we do not have a choice with regard to our early parental environment or our instincts, and according to social learning theories, we cannot choose which models we will be exposed to.

Evaluation of the humanist approach

One advantage of the humanist perspective generally is that it frees the personality psychologist from the bonds of determinism. Most of us feel that individuals do possess a certain amount of free will and that part of human nature is to strive towards higher goals. Humanist theories at least acknowledge this. However, it has been argued that the theories represent a philosophy of life and that they are not strictly speaking theories of personality. Moreover, as the self-concept is necessarily a subjective entity, phenomenological theories are not easily verifiable in accordance with standard scientific methods. Nevertheless, it is possible to investigate changes in people's self-perceptions and this approach has provided some empirical support for this aspect of phenomenological theories (Stephenson, 1953; Rogers and Dymond, 1954).

Different theoretical frameworks for understanding human individuality

Although theories which use an ideographic approach to the study of personality have chosen to focus on complete theories of individuality rather than on how one group of individuals differs from another group of individuals, they do not entirely reject the validity of making comparisons across groups. For example, it is still possible to ask what makes some people more aggressive than others, what makes some people have low self-esteem whereas others have high self-esteem or what makes some people act impulsively whereas others exhibit more behavioural restraint. Questions such as these, however, will generate different answers from theorists working within a psychoanalytic, social-learning or phenomenological tradition.

Most psychoanalytic theorists see aggression as a manifestation of pent-up aggressive energy directed outwards towards others, or inwards, in the case of self-inflicted acts of aggression (for example, Storr, 1970), whereas social-learning theorists view aggression as behaviour which has been modelled and reinforced (Bandura, 1977). In contrast with the psychoanalytic view, humanists believe that people are not by nature aggressive, and that aggressive behaviour therefore reflects one of the choices we make when we are unable to fulfil our creative potential. If a person can be given unconditional love, self-enhancement will be able to proceed unhampered and aggression will disappear as the person becomes progressively more self-fulfilled.

Self-esteem for the humanist theorist occurs as people get closer to achieving their perfectionist goals. The psychoanalytic view, however, sees self-esteem in terms of a history of ego-achievements. For instance, according to Erikson, the more conflicts at each of the psycho-social stages a person has resolved successfully, the higher that person's self-esteem. On the other hand, for the social-learning theorist, self-esteem can be seen as a history of positive reinforcement for behaviour.

The social-learning theorist might see impulsive behaviour in terms of behavioural inhibition/disinhibition which is governed by expectancies of reward and punishment based on past experience. The impulsive person expects to be rewarded for his/her behaviour, more often than punished for it. For the psychoanalytic theorist impulsiveness is the result of a failure to keep the demands of the *id* in check. The impulsive person is not fully able to delay gratification and his/her behaviour is therefore irrational and governed by his/her impulses. And according to phenomenological theories, behaviour which is a little impulsive is a good thing because it means we are acting to fulfil our individuality. Too much restraint prevents us from expressing our individuality and is therefore a negative thing. Thus, one of the characteristics of the fully-functioning person according to Maslow and Rogers is 'spontaneity'.

Summary

The psychoanalytic, social-learning and phenomenological approaches each attempt in different ways to explain how each of us is characterised by our own idiosyncratic patterns of behaviour. Whereas psychoanalytic views have their roots in the study of psychopathology and emphasise conflict and anxiety as the basis for individuality, social-learning theories focus on the learning environment and phenomenologists are concerned with the individual's present concept of self. Each approach has different implications when it comes to explaining personality. Even within the same perspective, individual theorists may adopt different philosophical positions with regard to issues such as whether people have free will, whether 'nurture' is a more important determinant of personality than 'nature' and whether it is valid to infer thought processes as determinants of behaviour. For example, it was argued in this chapter that Erikson's psychoanalytic theory is less deterministic than Freud's psychoanalytic theory and that whereas some learning theories have rejected 'thought' as a subject for study (e.g. Skinner), cognition has formed an integral part of other theories (e.g. Bandura).

Further reading

Hampson, S.E. and Colman, A.M. (eds) (1995). *Individual Differences and Personality*. Longman Essential Psychology series. A short paperback which contains chapters contributed by various psychologists working in the area of individual differences and personality psychology. Each chapter offers a different methodological focus.

Kline, P. (1984). *Psychology and Freudian Theory. An Introduction.* Methuen. An accessible paperback which expands on the description of Freud's ideas and gives a good critical evaluation.

Mischel, W. (1993). *Introduction to Personality*, 5th edn. Harcourt-Brace. Part II: Psychodynamic approaches; Part IV: Phenomenological approaches; Part V: Behavioural approaches. Most personality textbooks give an outline of the psychoanalytic, social-learning and phenomenological approaches to personality. Mischel's text offers a lively and easy to read account.

Measuring personality

IN CONTRAST TO THE IDEOGRAPHIC APPROACHES described in Chapter 3, which focus on how basic laws of human nature (instincts, laws of learning, motives for self-fulfilment) can give rise to *uniqueness* amongst individuals, **nomothetic** approaches emphasise *differences* between groups of individuals along specific personality dimensions. Nomothetic approaches assume that it is psychologically meaningful to compare individuals along specific personality dimensions because the basic laws which govern human differences in personality (rather than generalities in human nature) are themselves universal. The personality psychologist working from a nomothetic perspective attempts to first identify a number of personality dimensions which can be quantified or measured, then to compare and contrast groups of individuals according to their position on a particular personality dimension. This approach is also known as the **psychometric** or **trait** approach to personality.

Psychometric methods for personality measurement

The psychometric approach to personality follows from the assumption made by psycho-physicists such as Weber (see Chapter 2) that it is possible to measure aspects of human psychological functioning. The principle behind psychometric testing is that it is possible to quantify implicit characteristics of people through self-reports of their feelings, thoughts and behaviour. The tool used by psychometric psychologists to measure personality is the psychometric test. A psychometric test involves presenting subjects with a series of statements describing various ways of reacting or feeling. For example, the statement: 'I feel that I am not a person of equal worth to others' describes one way a person might feel, on a psychometric measure of self-esteem. Usually, subjects are asked to evaluate each statement according to how closely they feel that the description given applies to themselves, either by indicating whether they 'agree' or 'disagree' or by rating their response on a rating scale (for example: strongly agree, agree, neutral, disagree or strongly disagree). Subjects' responses to each item can then be quantified, for example, by scoring 'zero' for a 'disagree' response and 'one' for an 'agree' response, or, in the case of a rating scale, by scoring a '5' for a strongly agree response, '4' for agree and so on, down to '1' for strongly disagree. It is then possible to quantify the extent to which a person is characterised by a personality trait such as self-esteem by adding up their responses to each of the statements on the psychometric questionnaire.

The data from many psychometric measures from thousands of individuals' self-reports, or peer ratings of personality, along with observations of behaviour in naturalistic or laboratory settings, can then be used to ascertain the distribution of a trait in the general population. For example, we may find that some individuals are extremely sociable, most are quite sociable, others are not very sociable, and a few people are completely withdrawn. 'Sociability' can thus be represented as a personality dimension which has two extremes: sociable and unsociable. We can use the data to distinguish individuals from one another in terms of their sociability according to where their own sociability score is placed along the sociability dimension (this may be useful, for instance, if we would like to establish the likelihood that a particular person would be suited to a particular occupation for which a sociable nature is an advantage, say in careers guidance). We can also compare groups of individuals. For instance, we can compare aggressiveness scores in a population of young offenders with the aggressiveness scores of a comparable sample of young people who have no police record. Once we are able to describe individuals according to their scores on a number of personality dimensions, we can begin to discern a number of personality types. For example, people who are highly sociable and highly aggressive may belong to a 'sociable-aggressive' type, people who are highly sociable and unaggressive may belong to a 'sociable-unaggressive' type, people who are unsociable and aggressive may be classified as 'withdrawn-aggressive' and people who are unsociable and unaggressive may be classed as 'withdrawn-unaggressive'.

It is also possible to establish statistically the degree to which different psychological characteristics are related to each other. For example, it is possible to establish whether there is a tendency for sociability, aggression and self-esteem to go together, by correlating measures of each variable in large samples of subjects. The statistical technique used to establish the laws governing interrelationships between psychological characteristics is known as **factor analysis.**

Factor analysis: a statistical system for personality description

The method of factor analysis was first devised by Spearman (1904) to establish whether it is meaningful to distinguish between different forms of intellectual ability. Spearman wanted to know whether verbal ability, spatial skills, numerical skills and so on are independent of each other, or whether they all share something in common. Using the statistical technique for **correlation,** he inter-correlated measures of the performance of thousands of people on a variety of verbal, numerical and spatial tasks, and found that there was a positive correlation between the measures. That is, he found that a high score on one of the variables was associated with a high score on the other variables. Based on this research, Spearman concluded that the tests for verbal, numerical and spatial skills shared something in common: they each depended on some underlying general ability (a factor) which he called 'general intelligence' or 'factor g'.

This early research by Spearman led the way for a truly scientific methodology for studying implicit personality characteristics. Before Spearman, psychologists' descriptions of personality were more subjective. When Freud, for example, suggested that the anal personality is characterised by orderliness, parsimony and obstinacy, he had no way of statistically verifying whether people who are orderly are also obstinate, stingy and punctual other than his own experience of the covariation of these traits in his clients. Spearman's method, however, could be used to statistically establish the relationships between personality traits and thus psychologists' descriptions of personality were given an empirical basis. Moreover, *factor analytic techniques* meant that it should be possible to achieve a full scientific analysis of all of the personality traits used to describe individuals in everyday language, using a single accepted methodology rather than having to rely on several conflicting methodologies. If factor analysis is really able to quantify basic laws which govern human psychological functioning, then any psychologist using a factor analytic technique should come to the same conclusions about personality.

The factor-analytic method

Factor analysis is based on statistical tests of relationship called correlations. Correlations express the relationship between two variables according to the direction of the relationship: this may be positive, if scores on the two variables increase or decrease together (for example, the more it rains the faster plants grow); or negative, if as the scores on one variable increase, the scores on the second variable decrease (for example, the more it snows the slower plants grow); and the strength of the relationship is expressed as a number between +1 and −1 (for instance, +0.50 represents a strength in the middle of the scale, −0.75 a relatively strong correlation and +0.25 quite a weak correlation). If more than just two variables are tested, it is possible to obtain a *correlation matrix* which expresses all of the relationships between one variable and every other variable tested (a hypothetical correlation matrix is presented in Table 1).

In Table 1, we see that variables 1, 2 and 3 are all strongly related to each other in a positive direction, and that variables 4 and 5 are also strongly related to each other in a positive direction. On the other hand, variables 1, 2 and 3 are hardly related to variables 4 and 5 at all.

TABLE 1 Example of a hypothetical correlation matrix

	V1	*V2*	*V3*	*V4*	*V5*
			Variables 1-5		
Variable 1	1.00	0.90	0.88	−0.02	−0.08
Variable 2		1.00	0.85	0.07	0.00
Variable 3			1.00	0.00	−0.05
Variable 4				1.00	0.86
Variable 5					1.00

Factor analysis assumes that when variables are inter-correlated, they share something abstract or hypothetical in common: 'a *factor*'. (Thus, Spearman concluded that verbal skill, numerical skill and spatial skill must all be mediated by a fourth ability, 'factor g'.) In the example given in Table 1, we can see two possible factors emerging: factor 1 (which consists of variables 1, 2 and 3) and factor 2 (which consists of variables 4 and 5).

Of course, if we assume that variables are correlated to the extent that they share some hypothetical construct, or a *factor*, in common, then it follows that we should also be able to quantify the relationship between each variable and the *factor* itself. When this relationship is calculated statistically it is called a *factor loading*. Table 2 gives hypothetical factor loadings for five variables on two factors. The factor loadings suggest two factors: factor 1, on which variables 1, 2 and 3 load high and factor 2, on which variables 4 and 5 load high. In the interests of simplicity, all of the factor loadings represented are positive and none of the variables load negatively on the two factors.

We are now in a position to try to make psychological sense out of our hypothetical factors. In order to do this, we need to ask ourselves what it was that we measured in the first place. Let us assume that variable 1 represents an average time taken to complete various tasks; variable 2 represents self-reported concerns about the importance of meeting assignment deadlines (where a high score indicates more concern) and variable 3 represents peer ratings of punctuality (the higher the rating, the more

TABLE 2 Hypothetical factor loadings for five variables on two factors

	Factors	
	Factor 1	*Factor 2*
Variable 1	0.70	0.01
Variable 2	0.79	0.08
Variable 3	0.80	0.06
Variable 4	0.05	0.75
Variable 5	0.09	0.77

punctual the person). We might deduce from our factor structure that factor 1 represents a **trait** for conscientiousness, because factor 1 represents a tendency to take time over tasks, concern over deadlines and punctuality. If we further assume that variable 4 represents peer ratings of popularity (the higher the rating, the more popular the person) and variable 5, number of club memberships at college, we might deduce that factor 2 represents a trait for sociability. As factors 1 and 2 appear not to be related to each other, we can further assume that whether a person is sociable has little bearing on whether they are conscientious. Factors 1 and 2 in our example are thus said to be *orthogonal factors* (they are unrelated).

However, not all correlation matrices will give the clear pattern of correlations depicted in our hypothetical examples so far. Consider Table 3. Here, variables 1, 2, 3, 4 and 5 are all correlated. However, variables 1, 2 and 3 show stronger associations with each other than with variables 4 and 5 and variables 4 and 5 show stronger associations with each other than they do with variables 1, 2 and 3. Table 4 represents alternative factor loadings for five variables on two factors. In Table 4, all the variables load on both factors, however variables 1, 2 and 3 load higher on factor 1 than on factor 2 and variables 4 and 5 load higher on factor 2 than on factor 1. In such cases, it is usual for the researcher to define a criterion for factor loadings (a common criterion is + or −0.40; Kline, 1994). Only if the relationship between a variable and a factor exceeds the criterion, is the variable considered to load on the factor. If we highlight all the factor loadings in Table 4 which are above 0.40, then we again find that variables 1, 2 and 3 load on factor 1 and variables 4 and 5 load on factor 2. We therefore still have grounds for the conclusions reached previously, that factor 1 represents 'conscientiousness' and factor 2 represents 'sociability'. However, this time, conscientiousness and sociability are correlated because all of the variables which load on factor 1 are correlated with variables which load on factor 2. When two factors are related to each other, they are said to be *oblique factors*.

Oblique factors can be further factor-analysed by taking measures of each *primary* factor and then further inter-correlating

TABLE 3   Alternative correlation matrix for variables 1–5

	Variables				
	V1	*V2*	*V3*	*V4*	*V5*
Variable 1	1.00	0.90	0.88	0.40	0.37
Variable 2		1.00	0.80	0.29	0.19
Variable 3			1.00	0.20	0.35
Variable 4				1.00	0.90
Variable 5					1.00

TABLE 4   Alternative hypothetical factor loadings for five variables on two factors

	Factors	
	Factor 1	*Factor 2*
Variable 1	0.70	0.20
Variable 2	0.75	0.31
Variable 3	0.80	0.27
Variable 4	0.30	0.82
Variable 5	0.29	0.79

these until *second-order* factors emerge. For example, supposing the correlation matrix in Table 3 was larger and included many more variables, which gave factor loadings on four factors (conscientiousness, sociability, confidence and anxiety). We could then subject these factors to further inter-correlations by taking measures of the factors themselves, say by designing psychometric tests to measure each construct: 'conscientiousness'; 'sociability'; 'confidence'; 'anxiety' and so on. Then we could further inter-correlate people's scores on each test to yield second-order factors. For example, if 'sociability' and 'confidence' were positively correlated, we might call this factor 'assertiveness' and if 'anxiety' and 'conscientiousness' were positively correlated we might call this factor 'fear of failure'.

Factor-analytic studies of personality

A number of personality psychologists have used factor analysis to identify those personality traits which are most important to our understanding of the structure of personality. These studies typically use numerous measures tested on thousands of people and then subject the data to factor analysis in order to identify factors. Psychometric measures of the factors themselves may then be subjected to further factor analysis, in order to identify 'super-factors'. As all of the studies are essentially employing a similar statistical methodology, they should consistently reveal the same traits as emerging from the analyses. However, even a relatively well-defined methodology like factor analysis leaves room for researcher differences in how the methodology is applied. For example whereas Eysenck (1970) has emphasised a few orthogonal (unrelated) 'super-factors' (Eysenck prefers just three factors: extroversion-introversion; neuroticism-stability and psychoticism); Cattell (1965) favours a system of personality description based on 16 oblique personality factors. The differences arise because whereas some personality psychologists have ended their factor analysis at an earlier stage, others have preferred to merge several lower-level factors into 'super-factors'. Neither psychologist is 'right' or 'wrong', they are simply using alternative criteria for carrying their analyses further. Recall that where several variables are inter-correlated, it is possible to decide on a criterion or cut-off point for accepting factor loadings as significant and where different criteria are used, this will influence the eventual outcome of the analysis. Finally, the labels assigned to hypothetical factors which give them a psychological meaning are necessarily subjective. I decided to call 'factor 1' in the example given earlier 'conscientiousness', but factor 1 could equally have been labelled 'cautiousness' or even 'willingness to please others'. Differences in the ways in which personality researchers choose to label their factors can influence further factorisation of the trait measures themselves, by determining the sorts of items included in psychometric measures of those traits.

Despite the inevitable differences across psychometric psychologists, some factors do appear to emerge quite consistently from factor-analytic studies. For example, both Cattell (1965) and Eysenck (1970) describe factors which appear to tap extroversion/introversion and emotionality or anxiety, and personality psychologists appear to have reached a consensus that five personality factors may provide the best description of human personality (McCrae and Costa, 1987) although the five traits may be variously labelled. The five traits, sometimes called the 'Big 5' personality factors, are extroversion (or assertiveness, or impulse expression); agreeableness (or warmth or docility); conscientiousness (or will to achieve); emotionality (or neuroticism); and intellect (or openness to experience).

Trait theories of personality

The method of factor analysis has enabled personality psychologists to systematically extract the most important underlying temperaments which make up our individual personalities. Once these underlying dispositions or personality traits can be identified and measured, personality theorists can try to explain how the traits arise. They can then use measures of the personality traits to predict how people will behave across a variety of situations, in accordance with the assumption that people's behaviour in all kinds of situations should be similar to the extent that people share common underlying dispositions or personality traits (and different to the extent that they are characterised by different personality traits or dispositions).

Different explanations for the same personality traits

Researchers do not only differ in the ways in which they apply the factor-analytic method, they also differ with respect to the relative importance they attach to various trait dimensions derived from factor analysis. Gray's (1981) criticism of Eysenck's theory of extroversion/introversion and neuroticism/stability illustrates how different theorists can come to different conclusions about the importance of different personality traits.

According to Eysenck and Levey (1972) the trait dimension of extroversion/introversion has a physiological basis. It derives from inherited differences in the balance between excitation and inhibition within the cortex of the brain. According to Eysenck, as a result of this difference in physiology, some people are cortically 'over-aroused' whereas other people are cortically 'under-aroused'. Cortical arousal levels are also associated with conditionability. People who are cortically under-aroused are difficult to condition in conditioning trials, whereas people who are cortically over-aroused condition more easily. On the basis of this theoretical rationale, Eysenck makes a number of behavioural predictions. He hypothesises that people who are characterised by cortical over-arousal will try to avoid situations which involve too much stimulation; that is they will be 'introverts'. These individuals will prefer their own company to that of large groups and will not engage in activities which increase their levels of arousal. As cortical over-arousal is associated with good conditionability, introverts will condition easily and tend to think carefully before they take action which might be harmful. Alternatively, people who are under-aroused will seek stimulation in the form of company and excitement; they will be extroverts. As cortical under-arousal is associated with poor conditionability, extroverts will condition poorly and they are thus more likely to behave impulsively. In support of Eysenck, there is indeed evidence to suggest that extroversion is associated with a tendency to be sociable and to seek stimulation in the form of exciting activities such as fast or dangerous sports. Also, extroverts are more difficult to condition than introverts (Eysenck, 1970; Eysenck and Levey, 1972). Thus, according to Eysenck, impulsiveness and sociability are sub-components of the broader trait of extroversion.

Eysenck (1970) further assumes that neuroticism is a function of different inherited levels of autonomic system activity. An overactive autonomic nervous system results in emotional reactivity and behaviourally this will manifest itself in anxiety and neuroses. On the other hand, people who are not characterised by an over-active autonomic nervous system will be less emotionally reactive and their behaviour will be more emotionally stable. According to Eysenck, extroversion and neuroticism are orthogonal (or unrelated) factors, thus, whether you are neurotic does not influence whether you are extroverted, and vice versa.

However, other theorists have proposed alternative explanations for the status of extroversion and neuroticism as described by Eysenck. For instance, Gray (1981) has proposed his own theory of conditionability which has different implications. According to Gray, conditionability should be viewed in terms of a sensitivity to rewards on the one hand, and a sensitivity to punishments on the other. People who are over-sensitive to rewards are impulsive (they fail to inhibit their behaviour because they have high expectancies of being rewarded) whereas people who are over-sensitive to punishment are anxious (they inhibit their behaviour because they expect punishment). Individuals who are highly anxious and highly impulsive will display behaviour which is emotional because the combination of anxiety and impulsivity makes them react in an emotional way to most situations (these individuals are Eysenck's neurotics). On the other hand, whether people are extroverted depends on the relative strengths of their sensitivity to cues of reward and punishment. Someone who is more sensitive to reward than punishment will exhibit extroverted behaviour, whereas someone who is more sensitive to punishment than reward will exhibit introverted behaviour. Thus, according to Gray's conceptualisation, the traits of extroversion and neuroticism are by-products of the more important dimensions of impulsiveness and anxiety, whereas for Eysenck extroversion and neuroticism are the most important dimensions.

Gray is not the only psychologist to question Eysenck's view that extroversion and neuroticism are the most important traits governing individual differences in human behaviour. Plomin (1976), for instance, has argued that impulsiveness and sociability should be viewed as important traits in their own right, rather than as sub-components of the broader trait of extroversion.

Predicting behaviour from personality traits

Whereas trait theorists dispute the relative importance of different personality traits or factors and offer different explanations for the basis of personality traits, they do share a basic assumption about personality. All trait-based theories assume that personality is relatively stable. This implies that it should be possible to predict a person's behaviour in any situation given a knowledge of their personality. Traits (based on factors extracted using factor analysis) are therefore seen in terms of temperaments or underlying predispositions to behave in characteristic ways. For example, an extrovert should be more sociable, impulsive and sensation-seeking than an introvert, whenever we observe their behaviour, regardless of the context. We should not expect someone to behave in an extroverted way some of the time, and in an introverted way at other times if personality traits are truly important determinants of behaviour.

Some psychologists, however, have called into question the consistency of personality traits, arguing that personality traits are poor predictors of behaviour across situations. Mischel (1969) carried out a review of studies which have examined the relationship between different behavioural manifestations of various personality traits. For example, one of the studies cited by Mischel (Hartshorne and May, 1928) looked at lying, cheating and stealing in children as behavioural manifestations of a trait for 'dishonesty'. Mischel found that the statistical correlations between the different behaviours and a psychometric measure of the trait were relatively low (0.30 or less). He concluded on the basis of his review of the empirical evidence that personality traits rarely account for more than 10 per cent of the variance of behavioural events. In effect, Mischel was suggesting that personality traits are relatively unimportant determinants of behaviour.

Epstein (1977, 1979, 1983), however, disagrees with Mischel's conclusion that traits are unimportant and argues that Mischel's methodology is inappropriate. According to Epstein, Mischel was looking at the relationship between each personality trait measure and only one instance of each behaviour, whereas the truer test of cross-situational consistency would be to take several measures of each behaviour over time. In other words, Epstein suggested that we should use a principle of aggregation to assess cross-situational consistency, such as that used in a football or soccer league table. To establish whether a particular team is consistently good, we would not look at their performance on any one Saturday, because in all likelihood they would sometimes win, sometimes lose and sometimes draw. On the other hand, if we were to look at their average performance over the season (including the number of times they won and by how much, the number of times they lost and by how much) we would be more likely to pick out the best team. When Epstein applied an aggregate method to the issue of cross-situational consistency for a personality trait of 'cheerfulness' he found that whereas the relationship between self-reported cheerfulness and cheerful behaviour on any two occasions picked at random was low, when aggregate measures of cheerfulness were obtained, these were highly correlated with self-reports of 'cheerfulness' on a psychometric measure.

Epstein's approach, however, has been subject to counter-criticism. According to Mischel and Peake (1982), Epstein has missed the point, which is to predict related behaviours from a trait measure. Instead, they argue, he has only demonstrated that the same behaviour (cheerfulness) is consistent across situations. In other words, it would have been more appropriate to use a trait measure such as sociability to predict related behavioural measures (like cheerful behaviour, gregarious behaviour and excitement-seeking behaviour), rather than use a self-report of cheerful behaviour to predict actual cheerful behaviour. However, Epstein, in turn, rejects Mischel's approach on the grounds that any behaviours selected by Mischel as representative of a trait would be arbitrary: who is to say that cheerful, gregarious and excitement-seeking behaviours hang together as a trait, given that trait theorists themselves cannot always decide which clusters of behaviours represent personality factors (Epstein, 1983)? The current status of the debate over the cross-situational consistency of personality traits rests on whether we should expect trait measures to reliably predict a single example of behaviour over time, or whether we should expect traits to predict many different sorts of behaviours over time. This is an important issue as it has implications for whether it makes sense to assume that people behave in ways which are determined by stable temperaments or personality dispositions at all. If our behaviour is not determined by personality characteristics then obviously the study of personality is not a very useful way of trying to understand the causes of behaviour.

Summary

The *psychometric* approach to personality is based on methods for measuring implicit personality characteristics. This is a *nomothetic* approach to personality because it emphasises differences between groups of individuals along specific personality dimensions. The tools used by *psychometric* personality psychologists include *psychometric tests* and *factor analytic techniques*. Using factor analysis, personality psychologists have defined five personality dimensions which may be important determinants of human behaviour: extroversion, agreeableness, conscientiousness, emotionality and intellect (McCrae and Costa, 1987). However, differences in the ways in which the factor-analytic method is applied by researchers have given rise to disagreement regarding which traits are superordinate and which are subordinate, so that different theorists may have their own preferences regarding the relative importance of personality factors. Moreover, the process of labelling traits (or clusters of related behaviours representing factors) is still open to a degree of subjective interpretation. Nevertheless, trait theorists share the assumption of cross-situational consistency and a general criticism of trait theories is therefore that personality traits are not reliable predictors of behaviour across situations.

Further reading

See end of Chapter 5.

Personality traits or situations?

A T THE END OF CHAPTER 4 IT WAS suggested that one
assumption which is common to trait theories of personality
is the assumption of trait consistency. If personality traits are
important determinants of behaviour, then we should be able to
predict people's behaviour from a knowledge of their personality.
However, the assumption of personality consistency is not
confined to trait theories of personality. Any theory which assumes
that the ultimate causes of behaviour are temperaments or personality dispositions (i.e. that behaviour arises from stable internal
dynamics, processes or predispositions which exist separately
from situations) assumes that we should be able to predict how
people will behave across situations. This includes psychoanalytic
approaches, social-learning approaches and humanist approaches
to personality, as well as trait theories, because all of these
approaches assume that what we do reflects the sort of person
we are, more than the situations in which we find ourselves. As
we have already seen, we would not be able to talk about something called 'personality' if our behaviour was at the mercy of
external events, because the very concept of personality assumes
that people adopt consistent patterns of behaviour across all kinds
of situations. According to all approaches to personality, then,
our behaviour should be relatively consistent because it is determined by more or less stable temperaments.

However, some psychologists have suggested that we can
predict behaviour from a knowledge of situations. This view therefore denies that dispositions are important determinants of
behaviour and, if correct, may have important implications for
all of the major approaches to personality psychology.

Consider the following two examples of behaviour: (i) a
soldier firing at the enemy during wartime and (ii) a person sitting
quietly in church. Neither of these examples reveals very much
about the people's personality characteristics. Their behaviour is

more a response to the particular situations they are in. Sometimes a better explanation for our behaviour can be situational rather than dispositional. If we acknowledge situations as important causes of behaviour, then we should not expect personality traits to predict our actions. Instead, we would need information about the situation to predict our reactions. Some situations cause most people to react in remarkably similar ways. The following studies from social psychology illustrate the power which situations, and in particular social situations, can have over individuals' behaviour.

Social influence

Studies of obedience

In the early 1960s Milgram carried out an experiment in which he advertised in the press for volunteers from the general public to take part in a psychological study of learning at Yale University. On arrival at the laboratory, each participant was told by an experimenter dressed in a white lab coat that he was to play the role of 'teacher' and test another subject's memory for pairs of words. What the volunteers were not told was that the 'learner' in the experiment was a confederate of the experimenter. 'Teachers' were told that when the 'learner' got one of the word-pairs wrong, they were to press a lever which would deliver an electric shock to the learner. Each of the 'teachers' was asked to watch as the 'learner' was strapped into an electric chair in the next room. The teacher was then shown a shock generator panel with thirty lever switches labelled from 15 volts (mild shock) to 450 volts, clearly marked 'DANGER SEVERE SHOCK'. The experiment began, and each time the 'learner' wrongly recalled one of the word pairs, the experimenter instructed the teacher to administer the learner with a shock. The more mistakes the learner made, the higher the level of shock the 'teacher' was required to administer. As the level of shock administered by the teacher increased in intensity, the learner was heard to complain of being in pain. As the intensity of the shocks increased further, the learner would cry out, until at the highest intensities, the learner begged the teacher to stop administering shocks, he cried out, banged the wall and even complained that he had a heart condition. Despite the 'learner's protests and obvious distress, none of the participants in Milgram's study refused to administer electric shocks to the learner. An incredible 65 per cent of 'teachers' gave the full range of shocks as instructed by the experimenter even though the learner could be heard clearly to cry out in pain and beg for the experiment to end, and even though it was clearly marked on the shock generator panel that the highest intensity of shocks were dangerous. Moreover, not one of the participants stopped before they had administered a shock to the learner of at least 300 volts, by which time the learner was already showing signs of considerable pain and distress (Milgram, 1963).

Milgram's results apparently show that 65 per cent of a sample of average American adult men were willing to punish another person with increasing voltages of potentially dangerous electric shock when ordered to do so by an experimenter who did not possess any powers to enforce his commands. Milgram concluded that such a high level of **compliance** could not be attributed to personality characteristics of the individuals in his sample. These were average members of the public, who were neither particularly aggressive, nor particularly unfeeling. In fact, many of the subjects exhibited considerable distress in the laboratory, though they continued to carry out the experimenter's instructions. Instead, he concluded that the power of the situation was the most important determinant of the men's behaviour.

Milgram further demonstrated that people often underestimate situations as determinants of behaviour. When he described the experiment to a sample of students, he found that they predicted obedience rates of only 1.2 per cent and even a group of psychiatrists who were asked to predict the outcome of the experiment gave predictions of only 0.125 per cent.

None of the people who were asked to predict the behaviour of the subjects in Milgram's study came even remotely close to predicting the actual levels of compliance observed (Blass, 1991).

Milgram then repeated his study to see whether altering the situation itself would influence the levels of compliance obtained (Milgram, 1965). Modifications to the physical arrangements were indeed found to reduce compliance: for example, when the 'teacher' and 'learner' were in the same room, or when the experimenter gave instructions over the phone, compliance levels fell. Alterations to the social dynamics of the situation also reduced compliance: for example, when the status of the experimenter was reduced, by having him dress in ordinary clothes rather than a lab coat, or conducting the experiment in a down-town building, rather than at Yale University. These modifications to the situational determinants of compliance underline the power of the situation itself over the participants' behaviour. All people comply because all people have learned to display obedience to certain cues. The presence of an authority figure is associated with the power to punish, even when that power is not real. The people in Milgram's experiment were responding inappropriately to a situational cue which under other circumstances might be appropriate, and they did this despite, rather than because of, their own feelings or personal characteristics. In fact, when the cues denoting authority were reduced, by altering the way in which the experimenter and the situation were presented to the subject, compliance dropped. Also, when the subjects thought that they could get away without obeying the experimenter (such as when he gave orders over the phone) compliance also dropped.

Milgram's experiments show that some situations contain powerful cues which can maintain behaviour independently of people's personality characteristics. Aronson (1984) suggests that one definition of compliance is as behaviour which is motivated to gain reward or avoid punishment. However, the person's behaviour is only as long-lived as the threat of punishment or the promise of reward. He sees little difference between animals and humans in this respect. Consider the rat in Skinner's experiment. Skinner did not assume that the rat's behaviour was determined by its personality or temperament (whether in terms of cognitive expectancies, dynamics of conflict or personality traits). The rat's responses were determined by external events. In the Skinner box situation, behaviour is a response to situational cues (indeed, as a behaviourist, Skinner denied internal determinants of behaviour). Any rat will press a lever when cues are present which it has learned to associate with positive reinforcement (food) or negative reinforcement (the avoidance of pain) – when the light is switched on, when it hears a tone, after a time interval. If the cues associated with positive or negative reinforcement are removed, the lever-pressing behaviour ceases. Similarly, subjects in Milgram's experiment delivered shocks to the learner when cues associated with negative reinforcement by an authority figure were present. When the cues were removed, compliance dropped.

Studies of conformity

In other situations the cues which influence behaviour can be more subtle. Asch (1956) carried out a study in which he asked students to participate in a decision-making task. The experiment involved making judgements about whether stimuli presented to the participants were the same or different. People were tested in groups, and each person in turn was asked to make a decision regarding each stimulus. However, unknown to the participant, everyone in the room with the exception of themselves was a confederate of the experimenter. The stimuli used were simple: a series of three lines of different lengths. The participant was asked to pick out the line which was the same length as another 'target' line. The procedure was manipulated so that the participant always made their judgement after the other people in the room had reached a decision. Asch found that even when the decision was obvious, people were influenced by the judgements of others in the group, even when they had given an answer which was obviously incorrect. Even though they must have been certain of the correct answer, because the task was so obvious, they went along with the majority decision, against their better judgement. When Asch asked the participants in his study to account for their decisions after the experiment, they confirmed that they had thought that the rest of the group was wrong, but that they began to question their own judgement when faced with such unanimous contradiction.

Asch concluded that the pressure to conform to the group was powerful enough to override individuals' own judgements in his experiment. Explanations for the subjects' behaviour are sometimes given in terms of the subjects' desire to gain a reward in the form of social approval or by a desire to be like the group (identification) (Aronson, 1984). However, whatever the precise explanation for the subjects' behaviour, the social situation, rather than individual personality characteristics, emerges as the best predictor of how they behaved.

Aronson (1984) suggests that other social psychological phenomena can also be explained in terms of a conformity effect. For instance, studies of helping behaviour have demonstrated that witnesses to a crime or an accident are least likely to call for help when there are a large number of bystanders present. This effect is known as **bystander apathy**. Non-intervention in these situations appears to be determined by the situation, rather than by personality characteristics of the bystanders, because most of us, regardless of our individual dispositions, will fail to fetch help under these circumstances.

The power of situations

The social psychological studies described in the previous sections suggest that situations can often be more important than personality in explaining behaviour. Situations like the ones described above can create remarkable similarities in people's behaviour and tend to minimise individual differences. At least these studies imply that temperaments are relatively unimportant determinants of behaviour in some situations. However, some psychologists have argued that behaviour may be entirely maintained by external cues rather than by internal dispositions or personality characteristics. This view has come to be known as 'situationism' and one of the earliest proponents of situationism was Walter Mischel (1968).

The situationist perspective

According to Mischel, there is consistency in people's behaviour, but this consistency is best explained by regularities in external events, rather than by internal predispositions to behave in predictable ways. In its extreme form, therefore, this view represents an anti-personality theory, rather than a theory of personality. Mischel cites as evidence the fact that trait measures are poor predictors of behaviour (this issue was touched on in Chapter 4, but let us now look at it in more detail). As we have seen, Mischel argues that a demonstration of behavioural consistency, such as Epstein's finding that 'cheerfulness' is relatively consistent over time, only demonstrates that the cues which maintain cheerfulness were also present on all of the occasions in which Epstein took his measures. For Mischel, the true test of a trait is whether a temperament like 'sociability' measured on a psychometric test can predict related behaviours such as attendance of social functions, tendency to engage others in conversation and popularity with peers across situations; and according to Mischel, the evidence of studies such as that on dishonesty by Hartshone and May suggests that psychometric tests are indeed poor predictors of trait-related behaviours.

Mischel further argues that although we all perceive our own behaviour and that of others to be consistent, and although we use trait terms in language to describe behaviour as though it were consistent, in reality the trait terms we use in everyday language do not correspond to real differences and similarities between people. Instead, argues Mischel, traits are merely descriptive categories, similar to those which lead us to form stereotypes of behaviour. This effect can be seen in studies of impression formation, whereby our impression of a person can be influenced by information we are given about them. In a study by Asch (1946), for example, people gave different trait descriptions of an individual they had been interacting with, according to whether the experimenter introduced the person as having a 'warm' or 'cold' personality. It follows from this line of argument, that factor analytic studies of personality do no more than demonstrate that people (including psychologists) tend to group together behaviours in certain characteristic ways, not that we tend to behave in characteristic ways. According to Mischel, therefore, psycho-metric methods only 'pick up' the ways in which we view ourselves and others, not the ways we actually are.

The case against situationism

Personality psychologists have responded to Mischel's attack on dispositions by pointing out that if situational cues alone can be used to predict behaviour, then all people should behave in exactly the same way, as long as the cues present in a situation are the same. However, this is not always the case. For example, Blass (1991) has shown that even in a very well structured situation such as Milgram's experiment, individual differences are evident. Although 65 per cent of Milgram's subjects gave the full range of electric shocks, 35 per cent of the volunteers did give up before administering the final dose of 450 volts. Thus, although the situation would appear to be the best predictor of obedience, the best predictor of disobedience would appear to be disposition, because the situation was the same for all of the subjects taking part. Critics of situationism such as Blass are not suggesting that situations do not have important effects on our behaviour, rather they suggest that in order to predict behaviour, we need a knowledge of how people's personality characteristics and situations interact, because neither one alone is sufficient to account for how people behave in every context. Such psychologists have therefore proposed an interactionist perspective towards personality.

Interactionism

Interactionism represents a shift of emphasis within personality psychology. Instead of attempting to identify important person-ality traits or dispositional motivators of behaviour, interactionists focus on how situational variables moderate dispositional vari-ables. In other words, the focus is on identifying situations which maximise individual differences in personality and situations which minimise individual differences.

Situational moderators of personality

A number of writers have argued that three types of situation can override dispositional or personality attributes as determinants of behaviour (see Blass, 1991). These are strong rather than weak situations, chosen rather than imposed situations and situations which diminish rather than heighten self-awareness.

A strong situation is one in which the behavioural alternatives are limited. For example, Milgram's experiment is an example of a strong situation because the participants could only choose amongst two behavioural options: to continue giving electric shocks or to quit the experiment. Attempts to predict behaviour in a strong situation from personality measures typically fail, because the situation minimises individual differences. In fact, when the behavioural alternatives open to subjects are made less restrictive (for example, by allowing subjects to choose from amongst a range of shock intensities on each trial in a Milgram type paradigm), some trait measures, aggressiveness for instance, do predict behaviour.

Imposed situations also minimise the influence of individual differences. When people are given little or no choice, most people behave in the same way. Obviously, most people will obey orders if they are being held at gunpoint. However, even in the absence of overt coercion, we may perceive our choice as limited under certain circumstances. For instance, when we have already committed ourselves to a course of action, it will be harder for us to choose to stop. In Milgram's study, the fact that the subjects had volunteered to take part may have reduced their perceived choice, as they had already made a commitment to the experimenter.

Finally, when a task involves a high degree of self-absorption, so that attention is focused on the details of the procedure, subjects may become less self-aware. That is, they are less likely to reflect on why they are doing what they are doing. The consequent reduction in self-awareness results in behaviour which becomes automatic, and determined more by external events than by dispositional characteristics. In Milgram's study, subjects may have been absorbed in reading out the questions and the mechanical details of operating the shock machine.

As well as attempting to categorise situations according to whether they will tend to minimise or maximise individual differences, some psychologists taking an interactionist approach have tried to establish whether particular personality traits are connected to particular settings. This approach is based on Allport's (1937) view that individual differences in behaviour will not emerge until the situational conditions are right. Thus, 'individual differences in sociability or intellectual curiosity, like individual differences in sweatiness, will not emerge until aroused by suitable environmental stimuli' (Kenrick *et al.*, 1990: 685). Kenrick *et al.* (1990) found evidence to suggest that certain settings are indeed more relevant to the expression of certain traits. For example, whereas a trait for 'dominance' was more evident in a sports setting, it was less evident in a religious setting. However, one obvious drawback with such an approach is that it relies on the researcher being able to divide up the types of setting which people encounter in everyday life in a meaningful and objective way. For example, Kenrick *et al.* themselves acknowledge that there may be an almost infinite number of ways in which we might label situations, at least as many ways as there are of labelling people.

Dispositional moderators of situations

If there are situational moderators of personality, it follows that another way of approaching the issue of personality–situation interaction is to look for dispositional moderators of situations. Indeed, Bowers (1973) argues that whilst people may have a limited choice when it comes to how they behave in some situations, people may exercise considerable choice when it comes to the sorts of situations which they typically choose to become involved with, and some studies have shown that personality variables can predict preferences for particular situations. Furthermore, it is possible that whether personality is cross-situationally consistent or inconsistent, may itself be an individual difference variable. In other words, consistency itself may be a personality trait.

Interactionism and personality

The influence of situationism on personality psychology has meant that few psychologists now try to explain behaviour purely in terms of temperaments or underlying personality dispositions. Instead, personality theorists try to predict how people will behave from a knowledge of both personality dispositions and situations. The assumption underlying an interactionist approach is that if we know enough about the effect of individual situations on behaviour, we should be able to predict when people are likely to behave in a manner which is consistent with their underlying personality and when their behaviour is likely to be inconsistent with their personality.

Though few psychologists today would argue with the aims of an interactionist approach to personality, most would agree that the task of establishing exactly how situations and temperaments interact to determine behaviour in all possible contexts is a tall order indeed. Nevertheless, one of the strengths of an interactionist approach is that it has focused attention away from general, abstract causes of behaviour such as personality traits towards an analysis of the characteristics of situations in the present. In an applied setting, this can be much more useful than a knowledge of individual differences in personality alone, whatever their basis.

Applied psychologists are much more often concerned with people's reactions to situations than they are with people's personalities. Consider the situation of a clinical psychologist who wishes to help someone readjust to everyday life following a breakdown after a major life event. According to Bentall, it is of little use to an applied clinical psychologist to know what his/her client's personality profile is, or whether his personality is usually consistent across situations, because 'it is often the inconsistencies in behaviour which are most striking' (1993: 307). In other words, people are usually referred to a clinician in the first place, because their recent behaviour does not fit with what they are normally like. Labelling the client as having a particular type of personality is unlikely to be particularly helpful when it comes to helping them to change their current behaviour. What matters is helping clients to adapt their behaviour to new situations and to help them to deal with situations they may encounter in the future.

In an applied setting it may therefore be more useful to establish how people perceive ongoing situations, than to look at their behaviour over many situations in the past. This is because many of the behaviours displayed by people that we would wish to alter are confined to particular contexts. For example, someone who exhibits symptoms of depression following a bereavement may be reacting to a situation that involves the death of a loved one, a situation they have never experienced before. Or a child may begin to bully other children when he moves to a new area, because he feels threatened in these new and unfamiliar surroundings. Similarly, a student may perform poorly at examinations because she has never had to face this form of performance evaluation, or an employee may begin to experience problems at work since the introduction into the workplace of a new type of technology. Of course, one could still argue that people who have these problems are different from people who are apparently able to cope with each of these new situations. However, we do not necessarily need to assume that they possess different personality traits which determine their responses to many situations, we only need assume that they see this particular situation in a different way. The study of how people think about situations, and in particular social situations, is called social cognition, and another approach to the study of individual differences is therefore to focus on alternative ways in which people might perceive and think about specific situations, rather than try to predict their behaviour across different situations, by inferring that their behaviour is caused by an underlying temperament or personality disposition.

Summary

Situations can have powerful effects on behaviour and sometimes external events are more important than personality or temperament when it comes to predicting how people will behave in a particular context. Some 'situationists' have even argued that personality itself may not exist. Instead, situationists suggest that consistencies in behaviour can be explained entirely in terms of regularities in external events or situations. This view, however, may not be able to account for why a few people nevertheless behave differently in situations which appear to be identical, such as in Milgram's experiment on obedience, where the situation was set up to be the same for all of the subjects. Critics of situationism have therefore suggested that an interactionist approach to behaviour may be more appropriate. Interactionists attempt to identify the relative contributions of dispositional and situational variables as determinants of behaviour. Such an approach may be more useful in an applied setting, because it focuses less on intangible causes of behaviour such as personality traits and more on people's perceptions of ongoing situations in the present.

Further reading (Chapters 4 and 5)

Blass, T. (1991). Understanding behaviour in the Milgram obedience experiment: the role of personality, situations and their interactions. *Journal of Personality and Social Psychology*, 60, 3, 398–413. An excellent and relatively easy to read critical review of Milgram's experiments on obedience, with a focus on personality.

Bowers, K.S. (1973). Situationism in psychology: an analysis and a critique. *Psychological Review*, 80, 5, 307–335. This journal review article is written in an academic style rather than a 'textbook' style, so it is a bit difficult to read. Nevertheless it offers an excellent in-depth critical evaluation of the trait–situation issue, though the author supports the trait perspective.

Carver, C.S. and Scheier, M.F. (1992). 2nd edn. *Perspectives on Personality*. Allyn & Bacon. Chapter 4: Types, traits and interactionism. (Offers an academically rigorous, yet readable introduction to trait psychology).

Deary, I.J. and Matthews, G. (1993). Personality traits are alive and well. *The Psychologist*. July. British Psychological Society. An excellent up-to-date review of the current status of personality psychology, with critical commentary from a variety of psychologists working in different fields.

Pervin, L.A. (1984). *Current Controversies and Issues in Personality.* 2nd edn. Wiley. Chapter 1: Am I me or am I the situation? A relatively impartial, rigorous and easy to read account of the issues surrounding the trait versus situation debate.

Chapter 6

Making
social decisions

PERSONALITY THEORISTS HAVE FOUND IT difficult to defend the assumption that the major determinant of individual differences is something called 'personality', because it has not been possible to establish that personality traits predict behaviour across different situations. A major reason for this is that psychologists have not been able to agree on how best to define and measure 'personality'. Thus whereas some psychologists have preferred to view personality in terms of clusters of related behaviours, critics of this position have argued that decisions about which behaviours cluster together to form personality traits are subjective and arbitrary. Consequently, it may be fruitful to examine an alternative approach to the study of individual differences.

It was mentioned in Chapter 1 that personality psychologists are not the only psychologists concerned with understanding individual differences. Cognitive psychology, an area of mainstream psychology concerned with investigating people's perceptual and thought processes in a variety of situations, has recently suggested an alternative framework within which to view the concept of personality and individual differences. This approach sees individuals as information processors and thus individual differences are described in terms of the different processes or strategies which we use to solve various problems including social problems. 'Personality' viewed from within a socio-cognitive perspective is thus seen in terms of the various 'information processing strategies' which individuals apply to different situations, particularly social situations. This approach therefore offers an alternative to the traditional view of personality as being made up of general temperaments or dispositions which underlie our behaviour in all or most situations. The cognitive approach to individual differences has most in common with Bandura's social learning theory amongst traditional personality psychology theories because Bandura has suggested that implicit expectancies (part of people's thought processes or cognitions) determine behaviour. However, whereas Bandura uses the general term 'expectancy' to apply to one aspect of people's cognitions (how we predict reinforcements and punishments), cognitive psychologists have described several aspects of people's cognitions in terms of the processes and strategies which people might use to make all kinds of decisions in all kinds of situations.

Situations and internal states

According to the arguments put forward in Chapter 5, the behaviour of Milgram's participants was determined largely by situational cues. This conclusion was based on evidence which shows that almost anyone will follow orders under the same circumstances, and because when the situational cues for obedience are altered, compliance levels drop. However, if we were to ask a witness to the experiment, or one of the participants themselves, to explain what was happening in Milgram's situation, it is unlikely that they would describe the behaviour of the volunteers as a simple response to situational cues. Instead, their explanations would be more likely to focus on the experience of the person and on his internal state during the experiment. Thus, they might form judgements about his emotional state (was he afraid of the consequences of disobedience?); his attitudes (did he dislike taking part in the experiment?); his motives (did he intend to cause harm to the learner?); and, of course, his personality (was he just an ordinary nice guy, or someone with an underlying aggressive streak or psychopathic tendency?). In other words, in everyday life people try to infer something about how the participants in a situation might perceive what is going on, and what they might be thinking, in order to explain people's behaviour.

Personal constructs

One of the first psychologists to suggest that to understand people's behaviour we should first try to understand how people perceive and interpret their social and physical world was George Kelly (1955). Kelly proposed a cognitive theory of personality which accounts for human individuality in terms of the unique processes which enable each of us to understand and interpret our world. His ideas were influenced by the philosophical tradition of constructive alternativism which asserts that there is no such thing as objective reality, reality only exists in people's subjective interpretations of events. According to Kelly, human beings are analogous to scientists in that they formulate hypotheses about reality and use these hypotheses to predict events.

Kelly's theory is based on the assumption that human beings use a system for categorising and ordering their world which results in a unique pattern or template by which we each construe events according to our own interpretation or experience of them. He called these individual patterns or templates **personal constructs**. Our use of personal constructs allows us to systematically make sense of any aspect of the external world by categorising events along a bi-polar dimension. An example of a personal construct would be 'good' versus 'bad' or 'intelligent' versus 'stupid'. Whereas a course of action might be construed as 'bad' or 'stupid' by one individual, the same behaviour might be construed as 'good' or 'intelligent' by someone else. Thus, a single event can be construed differently by different people according to which pole of the construct each of us uses to interpret it. An individual's view of the world at a given point in time is therefore determined by his or her unique construct system which consists of an infinite number of events ordered according to an infinite number of construct dimensions. According to Kelly, behaviour is motivated to control events in the world according to our interpretation of those events. However, as personal constructs are really hypotheses about the way the world works, they are dynamic and frequently updated. This means that events which have previously been construed as 'good' can be construed later on as 'bad' on the basis of new evidence which alters our hypotheses about those events. As our hypotheses about the world change, so does our behaviour.

Kelly was therefore one of the first cognitive personality psychologists, and his theory introduced a new focus on the study of individual differences by suggesting that it may be important to establish how people think about events before we can predict how they will react to events. If we acknowledge that behaviour is a function of the way in which we construe our world, then we are ready to adopt a new level of analysis in our understanding of personality. We can examine individual differences in the ways in which people think about situations with a view to explaining how they might behave differently in those situations, without necessarily inferring general differences in temperament to explain individual differences in behaviour.

However, as most of the situations which we encounter are social situations and our behaviour in social situations is often a response to the behaviour of other people, we first need to examine some of the cognitive strategies available to all human beings by which we might attempt to make sense of the behaviour of others.

Situations or dispositions, that is the question

One important aim in trying to understand the causes of the behaviour of others is to establish whether their behaviour is dispositional (i.e. caused by their personality) or situational (caused by cues present in the situation). Lay people may therefore share the same aims as personality psychologists, in that both may be concerned with distinguishing between whether a particular behaviour is caused by internal or external events. However, the ability to make this distinction is especially important in everyday life. For instance, if someone were to push you over in the street, it would not be particularly useful to retaliate aggressively if their behaviour was perceived as accidental (i.e. caused by some external event such as their tripping up on an uneven paving stone), whereas it would be adaptive to prepare to defend yourself against a further attack if you concluded that their behaviour was an act of aggression (they meant to push you). In this situation, no doubt, you would quickly look for cues present in the person's facial expression, body language, or the reactions of others present, to help you to decide whether the person who pushed you meant to cause you harm. Only when you decide that they did not intend any harm would you decide that their behaviour was accidental (and therefore situational). Theories of social cognition which attempt to explain how we infer the causes of behaviour in everyday settings are called attribution theories. There is a sense in which attribution theories are therefore really lay theories of personality, because they seek to establish the causes of behaviour in terms of dispositional attributes. Only when it is possible to rule out dispositions as a cause of behaviour, will the cause of the behaviour be viewed as situational.

Theories of causal attribution

Heider (1958) was one of the first psychologists to recognise that people see behaviour as attributable to either the person or the situation. According to Heider, we use two sorts of information to help us to decide whether the person is the ultimate cause of any behavioural act. First, we seek cues to establish whether the behaviour involved 'effort' on behalf of the actor (the person carrying out an action), and whether the actor had the 'ability' to carry out the behaviour concerned. If we conclude that effort and/or ability are involved then we will attribute the behaviour to the person, whereas if we deem that effort and ability are not involved, then we attribute the behaviour to some external or situational event. For example, when someone passes an examination, we might look for evidence to suggest whether they worked hard towards the exam (effort) and whether they appear to be intellectually able (ability). If we conclude that they are not particularly able and that they did not work hard towards the exam, we might decide that their exam pass was due to luck or biased marking (both external or situational variables).

Since Heider, a number of alternative models of attribution have been proposed, each of which attempts to identify how we use information to decide on the causes of behaviour. These theories vary according to the sorts of information they assume is important in reaching causal attributions, but also according to their assumptions about how systematically we approach the task. Three important theorists in the area of attributional psychology are Harold Kelley (1973) and Jones and Davis (1965).

People as social scientists

According to Kelley (1973), the processes we use to establish the causes of people's actions in everyday settings are the same as those used by social scientists to empirically establish causality in scientific experiments. In other words, like social scientists, we look for relationships (or correlations) between events in the social world, and we try to establish the degree to which events co-vary. Our approach to identifying the causes of any behaviour is therefore highly systematic and follows the same rules we have seen used by personality psychologists previously. Given any behavioural event, we seek to establish three things: first, is the behaviour distinctive, or unique to a specific situation? (in other words, to what extent is the behaviour either cross-situationally consistent, or only elicited by specific situational cues); second, is the behaviour consistent over time? (to what extent are our observations of the behaviour replicable or reliable across similar situations on different occasions); and third, we would seek information about consensus (do most people exhibit the same behaviour in this situation, or does the behaviour tell us something about the individual concerned?). Whether we perceive that a particular behaviour is dispositional or situational will depend upon the inferences we make based on these three types of information. For example, we may conclude that someone who reacts to the loss of their job by becoming depressed is showing behaviour which is distinctive (they are not usually depressed and are only depressed due to their job loss). We might then ask whether they would react in this way to the loss of any job at any time, or whether their behaviour is a response to specific circumstances (they loved this job; they are already in financial difficulty). Finally, we would seek to establish whether other people are likely to respond to the loss of a job in the same way, under the same circumstances (we would seek consensus information). If we concluded that the person is depressed because of the loss of their job under difficult financial circumstances and that anyone else would react in the same way, we would be making an external or situational attribution. On the other hand, if we concluded that the person is often depressed, or that they always react to similar set-backs by becoming depressed, in a way that most other people would not, then we would be making a dispositional, or internal attribution. According to Kelley, therefore, we attempt to determine the extent to which a behaviour is caused by aspects of the person or the situation by inferring the distinctiveness, consistency and consensus of their behaviour in relation to situational events.

A critical evaluation of Kelley's model

One of the strengths of Kelley's approach over that of Heider is that whereas for Heider we are only interested in establishing the causes of behaviour as either due to the person or the situation, Kelley's model allows for more subtle attributions of causality. For example, using the three dimensions of distinctiveness, consistency and consensus we can adopt an interactionist perspective. Thus, Kelley's model allows us to distinguish between behaviour which may be caused mostly by personality traits (if the behaviour is low on the distinctiveness dimension, high on consistency and low on consensus) and between behaviour which is the result of a person–situation interaction (if the person's behaviour is highly distinctive, highly consistent, but low on consensus).

However, Kelley's model has been criticised because when people are asked to make causal attributions regarding ongoing behaviour in a naturalistic setting, they do not always consider the distinctiveness, consistency and consensus of behaviour. In fact, studies have found that whereas people often request distinctiveness and consistency information they are not particularly interested in consensus information (McArthur, 1972). This may imply that people do not request some types of information because they believe that they already have the answers themselves. Kelley subsequently modified his original theory to allow for the possibility that people have their own preconceptions about the distinctiveness, consistency and consensus of behaviours and suggested that they may select from their own store of hypotheses when making attributions instead of basing their inferences on actual observations (Eiser and Van der Pligt, 1988). If people do indeed impose their own preconceptions on the situation, rather than use cues which are actually present, this implies that the process of attribution is far from being the systematic and scientific process which Kelley originally assumed, and that it is based instead on a degree of subjectivity.

Jones and Davis's model of attribution

An alternative to Kelley's model of attribution is that of Jones and Davis (1965). According to Jones and Davis, our judgements about the causes of behaviour are based on inferences about whether the person is responsible for their actions (i.e. whether they intended the outcome of their behaviour), rather than on observations of the covariance of behaviour and situational events. In order to establish intention we use two types of information: we try to establish whether the person had knowledge of the consequences of his actions; and we try to establish whether the person had the ability to carry out the behaviour. Jones and Davis use the terms 'correspondent inference' to describe an attribution whereby the outcome of behaviour is judged to be intended, and 'non-correspondent inference', where the outcome of behaviour is judged as unintended. Thus, if someone is judged to have the knowledge and ability to carry out a behaviour, we make a correspondent inference. For example, if you saw someone walk away from the baggage collection point at the airport with your suitcase, you would want to establish whether they knew that the case was not their own (knowledge) and whether they seemed like a person capable of theft (ability), before you called the police. If you found that the person mistakenly believed the case to be their own, or that the person turned out to be an elderly person who was obviously confused and disoriented, you would probably conclude that they did not intend to steal your case and were not therefore responsible for their actions. On the other hand, if they appeared to know perfectly well that they had the wrong case, and you thought them capable of theft, you would report that a crime had taken place.

Therefore, whereas Kelley assumed that in making causal attributions, people are similar to social scientists, according to Jones and Davis, people could be considered to operate like attorneys of law, because like an attorney, we are interested in whether people are responsible for their behaviour, as well as whether their actions were caused by dispositional and situational variables. The following example illustrates this distinction. Suppose you gave a herbal remedy to someone who was feeling unwell, and they died as a consequence. Nobody could deny that you were the cause of their death because your behaviour was instrumental in bringing their death about. However, whether you were responsible for their death would depend upon whether you were aware that the remedy could cause death and whether you intended to use it in this way. Of course, establishing intention and therefore responsibility whether in real life, or in a court of law, is not a precise science. We may be swayed by certain types of information, to which we give more weight in reaching a decision. This is acknowledged by Jones and Davis who consider that people are biased towards making a correspondent inference under certain conditions. For example, when somebody's behaviour is unconventional or socially undesirable, or when their actions affect us personally, we are more likely to make a correspondent inference, and hold people responsible for their behaviour. This tendency implies that people's decisions about the causes of other people's actions and their consequences are not always completely rational and are subject to bias.

Attributional biases

According to Jones and Davis, the implicit lay theories of personality which help us to establish the causes of other people's actions are not as systematic and scientific as Kelley originally suggested. So how far can we trust our own judgement when it comes to establishing the reasons behind people's actions, if those judgements are based on preconceptions and biases rather than on evidence? Some psychologists have put forward the radical proposal that the attributional process is not really based on a systematic consideration of the evidence present in situations at all. Indeed, our decisions about the causes of other people's behaviour may be entirely based on heuristics or cognitive biases. This means that the whole process is seen as automatic rather than systematic.

The Fundamental Attribution Error

According to Nisbett and Ross (1980) people's decisions about causality are biased towards the person and we typically ignore situational determinants of behaviour. Nisbett and Ross believe that people neither have the time to make carefully considered judgements of causality, nor are they willing to expend much effort on the process. Instead, we use short-cuts or **heuristics** to decide about causality in an automatic way. As these heuristics favour dispositional rather than situational variables, we are always more likely to blame people for the consequences of their actions, and we ignore situational determinants of behaviour. This leads us to commit what Nisbett and Ross called a **Fundamental Attribution Error** (or FAE).

According to Nisbett and Ross, the simple rules or heuristics we apply to establish the causes of behaviour are derived from the ways in which we organise information about the world. In other words, just as Kelly suggested that we impose a structure on what we perceive, Nisbett and Ross suggest that we selectively extract information from situations by following well-established rules for the organisation of information. For example, we may group together information which is similar or which reminds us of previous situations (the representativeness heuristic); we may base our decisions about causality on whatever information comes to mind first (the availability heuristic); and we may prefer to select

information which confirms rather than disconfirms our expectations (the confirmation bias heuristic). In applying these rules, we
inevitably conclude that people are responsible for their actions
because information about people and behaviour is grouped
together (not information about people and situational cues); thus
people resemble actions more than situations. Moreover, we will
ignore consensus information as this is unlikely to spring to mind
rapidly and situational cues are pallid or boring compared with the
vivid image of someone's actions.

Evidence suggests that people do indeed demonstrate a
tendency to commit the FAE. For example, this appears to be
exactly what people are doing when they blame the 'teacher' for
his behaviour in Milgram's experiment, rather than the situation
(recall that studies in which people were asked to estimate how
many people would deliver an electric shock to the learner
produced very low estimates of compliance) (Elms and Milgram,
1966). Other studies too suggest that we tend to blame people
for their behaviour rather than situations across a variety of
everyday contexts, for example Nisbett and Borgida (1975), Wells
and Harvey (1977). What is more, so compelling is our tendency
to attribute the consequences of people's actions to people's dispositional attributes or personality traits that we frequently hold
people responsible for random or chance events such as winning
a lottery, the outcome of which they could not possibly have
caused (Langer, 1975).

How fundamental is the Fundamental Attribution Error?

People certainly appear to commit the fundamental attribution
error. However, do they always use short-cuts or heuristics which
favour persons and dispositions over situations? The answer to
this question appears to be that they do not. In some situations,
people are more likely to attribute the causes of behaviour to situational factors rather than dispositional ones. For instance, Jones
and Nisbett (1972) found that whereas observers of a situation
did tend to make attributions in terms of disposition, in line with
the FAE, actors (the people who were involved in the situation)

tended to attribute their own behaviour to external or situational variables. In other words there was an actor–observer divergence in attributions of causality. One reason for this is that actors may be more aware of cues present in the situation than observers. Additionally, actors may have information about the consistency of their own behaviour in other situations, which an observer does not have. Zuckerman (1979) also reported a situation in which people did not always commit the FAE. He found that actors will attribute variously to the person or situation depending on whether the outcome of their behaviour has positive or negative consequences. People therefore appear to operate a self-serving bias in making attributions, whereby positive consequences of their behaviour are attributed to their actions ('I got the job because I am a good salesperson') whereas negative consequences are attributed to outside influences ('I did not get the job because the interviewer was prejudiced against me').

The phenomena of the actor–observer divergence and the self-serving bias suggest that there may be limitations on when people will commit the FAE. However, some cross-cultural studies have called into question the extent to which the Fundamental Attribution Error is really as fundamental as Nisbett and Ross suggest. In a review of studies, Zebrowitz (1990) noted that the FAE is not reliably observed across cultures. In fact, whereas in the West people do tend to make dispositional attributions, in the East (Korea, Japan) people favoured situational attributions of causality. This would appear to suggest that the FAE may represent one strategy for attributing causes to people's behaviour (which happens to be that favoured in the Western world) rather than the only strategy and an inevitable consequence of human cognitive information processing.

Cognitive biases in thinking and deciding

Attributional judgements about the causes of behaviour are not the only decisions which human beings must make in the course of their everyday lives. People constantly find themselves in a variety of problem-solving situations, from choosing which job offer to accept, to deciding which route to take on a car journey. Cognitive psychologists have investigated the accuracy of people's judgements in a variety of situations, and have discovered that people's decisions about all kinds of events are subject to biases (Baron, 1995).

Some of the heuristics we have already encountered in relation to attributions of causality also apply to problem-solving in other contexts. For example, the availability heuristic, the representativeness heuristic and the confirmation bias heuristic have consequences for all sorts of decisions, because they determine the sort of information we will select (and reject) in coming to a conclusion, regardless of the appropriateness of such information to an effective solution. Other biases can be seen to operate in relation to our judgements about the relationship between events, and choosing amongst alternative courses of action. In particular, studies have shown that people have a tendency to misjudge the probability of events.

Judging the relationship between events

In order to judge the relationship between events accurately, it is necessary to estimate the likelihood of each event's occurrence and the likelihood of both events occurring together. This can be calculated mathematically as a probability. For example, taking a large number of samples it is possible to note how often various outcomes occur. So, the mathematical probability of landing 'heads' or 'tails' on tossing a coin is 1 chance in 2, or 50 per cent on each trial. Over a large number of trials, 'heads' will come up on half the tosses and 'tails' on half the tosses. To calculate the probability of 'heads' coming up twice in a row, the probability is calculated by multiplying the chances of tossing 'heads' on each trial: the probability is therefore $1/2 \times 1/2 = 1/4$ (or 25 per cent).

However, in real life, unlike in science or mathematics, people do not have the opportunity, or time, to systematically record the occurrence of every event we encounter. We therefore must subjectively estimate the likelihood of an event based on past experience and educated guesses. This process of estimating probability subjectively has been called subjective probability (Eiser and Van der Pligt, 1988). We use subjective probability all the time to estimate events such as our chances of landing a particular job before and after attending the interview, the likelihood that it will rain when we have left our umbrella at home, or the chances of getting stuck in a traffic jam when driving to a holiday destination. But how accurately are we able to assess the actual probability of events, using subjective judgements of probability?

In a variety of studies on the accuracy of people's subjective judgements of probability, Kahneman and Tversky (1972) found that people were not very accurate. For example, people tended to use heuristics in judging probability which were based on spurious relationships between situational variables. For instance, asked to estimate whether the chances that all of the births on one day in the maternity wing of a hospital would be males would be greater in either (a) a very large hospital or (b) a very small hospital, subjects tend to answer that this event is more likely in a large hospital. However, unusual events are much more likely to occur in a small sample so, mathematically, it is more likely that all the births in the small hospital would be males on any one day. It seems that the subjects in Kahneman and Tversky's experiment were swayed in their decision by the tendency to associate unusual events with 'largeness', a strategy which has nothing to do with mathematical probability and which is bound to mislead. In other words, the strategy they used to intuitively judge the correlation between two events (all the births being males, and a large or small hospital) was abstracted in a subjective way and did not follow the rules of mathematical probability. In a further study by Smedslund (1963), nurses were asked to estimate whether there was a relationship between a particular symptom and a particular disease. The nurses were provided with cards representing excerpts from the files of patients which indicated for each patient whether the symptom was present or absent, and whether the disease was diagnosed as present or absent. In reality there was no relationship between presence or absence of the symptom and the disease. In fact, of 70 patients with the symptom, 37 had the disease. Whereas, out of 30 patients who did not have the symptom, 17 had the disease. Smedlund found that 85 per cent of the nurses tested said that there was a relationship between the disease and the symptom. In reaching this conclusion, the nurses appeared to be basing their judgements on the number of patients in whom both the symptom and the disease were evident, but ignored those patients who exhibited symptoms in the absence of the disease, those who were diagnosed as having the disease in the absence of the symptom and those who had neither the symptom nor the disease. This study therefore demonstrates that our subjective judgements of probability may follow different rules to mathematical probability, even when we are given sufficient data to make an objective decision.

Choosing amongst alternative courses of action

Most of the decisions which we make in real life involve more than just estimating the likelihood of events. We try to control outcomes based on our predictions. This means that we hope to increase our chances of experiencing good events and decrease our chances of experiencing bad events. When we choose a particular course of action, therefore, our decision will involve an estimate of the likely result of acting in this particular way, compared to alternative courses of action. However, it will also involve an evaluation of the value of the different possible outcomes. That is we not only ask: 'what are the chances of "x" happening rather than "y"?', but also: 'how much would I like for "x" to happen, and how much would I like for "y" to happen?'. When we have established the likelihood of each event, and estimated the value we attach to each event, then we can choose the outcome which is most attractive to us, whilst avoiding outcomes which are most aversive.

Another way of looking at it is to say that the expected consequences of people's decisions are estimated based on costs and benefits to the person. This idea comes from economics (see Baron, 1995; Eiser and Van der Pligt, 1988). In the world of objects, the value of something is determined by its actual worth (in currency) and its subjective value (its worth to an individual). Thus, a tin ring may be worth little or nothing in monetary terms, but it may be worth a great deal to someone if it has sentimental value to them. The term 'utility' is often used to differentiate objective value (actual worth) from subjective value (subjective worth). Eiser and Van der Pligt (1988) use the following example to illustrate the term 'utility': if a poor person and a rich person both win £100 at the racetrack, the monetary value of their win is identical, but the subjective utility of this win to the poor person is much greater than it is to the rich person.

A number of psychological models of decision making have tried to take into account the concepts of subjective probability and subjective utility. These can be sub-categorised according to whether they adopt a normative or descriptive approach. Normative approaches try to specify how decisions should be made, whereas descriptive approaches aim to describe how people actually make decisions. According to the normative approach, people should operate a set of rules for combining beliefs about the occurrence of events (probabilities) and preferences (utilities) to make a decision. According to Subjective expected utility theory, people ought to follow the stages listed below in choosing amongst alternative courses of action (Eiser and Van der Pligt, 1988):

1   List all feasible courses of action.
2   Enumerate the possible consequences for each action.
3   Assess the attractiveness or aversiveness (utility) for each consequence which might occur.
4   Assess the likelihood that each course of action will result in a positive or negative consequence.
5   Compute the expected utility of each consequence by multiplying its utility by its probability of occurrence.
6   Choose the action with the greatest expected utility.

However, people do not appear to behave according to this model. Instead, descriptive approaches, which investigate how people actually make decisions, suggest that people do not always select courses of action according to the mathematical probability of their outcomes (Kahneman and Tversky, 1979). For example, people tend to view events with a high probability as certain, so that they do not differentiate between a probability of 80 per cent and one of 100 per cent. Whereas events with a low probability may be either ignored (as in deciding that it is very unlikely that you will be involved in a traffic accident, so you do not take out life insurance) or over-weighted (such as believing that it is worth insuring your home against a freak accident or believing that you will win the national lottery). People also attach more weight to losses than they do to gains and will do more to avoid an undesirable event than they will to gain a reward. For example, if someone gave you £40, and you lost £10, you would consider this to be worse than if someone had simply given you £30, even though you end up with the same amount of money.

These findings suggest that people do not always choose optimum solutions when faced with a problem. In fact, they exhibit anomalies of preference which do not fit with rational models of decision making and they may either take chances (gamble) or avoid risks in a way which is not consistent with mathematical probability. Findings such as those described above have led some psychologists to suggest that people may not actually be interested in optimum solutions at all, in fact most of us may be satisfied with solutions which are 'good enough', rather than seek the optimum solution (Simon, 1957).

Situations, decisions and individual differences

If people reasoned in a completely rational or systematic way this would inevitably lead to them choosing an optimum course of action for every situation they encountered, and identical situations should provoke identical reactions from all individuals. Like computers which have been pre-programmed with a set of instructions which follow well-defined scientific or mathematical rules for solving problems, we should all come to the same conclusions about how to respond to the cues present in a situation. We have already seen, however, that this is not the case, and even in highly structured situations, such as Milgram's experiment, people exhibit differences in behaviour. One way of looking at individual differences within situations is to assume that people may exhibit differences in behaviour in the same situation, to the extent that they use different rules for making decisions about what is going on. Once we acknowledge that people do not always take the most rational course in choosing how to behave, we can try to identify various strategies which people do use in a variety of situations, and then see whether some people tend to prefer some strategies more than other people. We can then try to predict which strategies will tend to be associated with particular behaviours or courses of action, and which strategies lead to more or less effective solutions.

Summary

People use a variety of cognitive strategies to help them to make decisions in their everyday lives. Attribution theories attempt to explain the process by which people make inferences about the causes of people's actions and the consequences of their actions. However, different theories of attribution make different predictions about this process of inference. Thus, whereas Kelley assumes that we approach the task in a systematic, rational and scientific way, Jones and Davis suggest that our attributional judgements may be subject to certain biases. On the other hand, Nisbett and Ross have argued that the attributional process is far from rational, and is more 'automatic' than 'systematic'. People's reasoning and problem solving in other situations may also be subject to heuristics or biases in information processing. For example, whereas normative theories of decision making such as subjective expected utility theory suggest that we should be able to compute the most effective solution to a problem, and thus choose a course of action which maximises our chances of the best solution, descriptive studies suggest that in reality, people do not always adhere to rational rules in selecting amongst behavioural alternatives. Human beings may therefore adopt a variety of strategies in making decisions about how to behave in different situations, and some people may prefer to use some strategies in some situations, whereas other people may prefer different strategies.

Further reading

Baron, J. (1995). *Thinking and Deciding*. 2nd edn. Cambridge University Press. (Especially Part II, on probability and belief). This book goes beyond the basic cognitive heuristics mentioned in this chapter and is for anyone who would like to read further.

Hewstone, M., Stroeber, W. and Stephenson, G.M. (eds) (1996). *Introduction to Social Psychology*. 2nd edn. Blackwell. Part II: Construction of the social world (Chapters 5, 6 and 7). These three chapters offer a clear and relatively comprehensive overview of the social-cognitive approach including the main theories of attribution. Each chapter is written by a different author who specialises in research in the field.

Personality or cognitive styles?

STUDIES OF SOCIAL COGNITION suggest that human beings use a number of cognitive strategies for making sense of social situations and for predicting the outcome of future events. What is more, the strategies which we use to make sense of our social world are not necessarily very rational or very systematic; in other words the strategies we adopt to make sense of a situation are not necessarily those suggested by the situation as being most likely to benefit us. If we all behaved rationally, presumably we would all reach similar conclusions on the basis of the same available information. Instead, the evidence suggests that we may interpret the same information in different ways because each of us uses a slightly different strategy to process the same information. This is the view taken by Sternberg (1995) who suggests that individuals may be distinguished according to their preferred ways of using their cognition. According to Sternberg, all individuals possess the ability to make sense of and function adaptively in the situations which they encounter throughout their lives. However, they may use this ability in different ways, resulting in individual differences in what Sternberg refers to as 'cognitive styles' or 'thinking styles'. The main difference between a cognitive style and a temperament or personality disposition is that whereas a cognitive style represents a cognitive strategy which can be defined in terms of some desired outcome, temperaments are not usually defined in terms of their outcomes. The following example illustrates this distinction. Suppose that you are a general in charge of an army, and you give your soldiers an order to advance on the enemy. Your order to advance may represent a cognitive decision based on your assessment of the situation. In other words, your decision to advance represents part of a strategy for producing a desired outcome (defeat of the enemy). Given a different set of circumstances, however, you might adopt a different strategy (you might decide that it is more prudent to wait until nightfall before calling your soldiers forward). Further-more, although your decision to advance may be a strategic deci-sion, not everyone might agree with your choice of strategy. Another general might take a different decision given the same circumstances. On the other hand, if you give the order to advance because you are bored with waiting around, your behaviour would not form part of a particular strategy and your action would be carried out without a particular outcome in mind. In which case it might make more sense to describe your behaviour as disposi-tional (or temperamental).

Another distinction between a temperament and a cognitive style is that whereas temperaments imply that our behaviour should be consistent across many, if not most, situations (a general who displays impatience on the battlefield is likely to behave impa-tiently when standing in a bus queue or in a traffic jam), cognitive styles may or may not lead to consistencies in behaviour across situations, because the particular strategy or style which we prefer will depend on the specific context. Behaviour will therefore only be consistent across several situations if we perceive that each of these situations demands the same strategy or approach. Theories of cognitive style have therefore tried to describe and predict individual differences in thought and behaviour within specific situations, in terms of the various ways in which we might prefer to process particular sorts of information, without necessarily inferring broad differences in temperament between people. The remainder of this chapter reviews research and theories which have described various cognitive styles in relation to different kinds of situational contexts in social psychology, cognitive psychology and applied psychology.

Cognitive styles in a social setting

Social theories of cognitive style have suggested a number of cogni-tive styles which people use in social situations. For example, Adorno *et al.* (1950) proposed that some people adopt a rigid information processing style when processing information about other people. Such individuals are intolerant of ambiguity and tend to hold rigid stereotypes, which lead to prejudiced behaviours. Adorno referred to individuals who think in this way as 'authoritarian personalities' because their cognitive style leads them to adopt conventional beliefs, to be intolerant of weakness, highly punitive, suspicious of anyone who is non-conformist and unusually respectful towards authority. A similar approach was taken by Rokeach (1954) who proposed that individual differences exist in 'dogmatism', the tendency to dislike new ideas. According to Rokeach, individual differences in dogmatism may arise because of differences in the ways in which people organise information about social values; thus individuals who are dogmatic prefer to use more rigid categories for organising information about social values in memory. As this type of categorisation is inflexible, this can lead to intolerance towards alternative attitudes or behaviours.

Attending to internal or external events

Other researchers have suggested that there may be cognitive styles associated with individual differences in attending to internal events or external events. According to Witkin et al. (1954), individuals may vary according to how they select information when making perceptual judgements. For instance, when judging whether a rod is vertical it is possible to use two strategies: we can compare the rod with some other object in the environment or we can use internal cues, such as cues made available by the position of our own body in space. In his experiments, Witkin discovered that people may use either strategy. Thus, whereas some people relied on internal cues (a field-independent style), others preferred external cues (a field-dependent style) in judging the verticality of the rod. Subsequent research has demonstrated a relationship between field dependent or independent styles and problem solving behaviour in social situations. Thus, field-dependent people attend more to social cues in the environment (people information) than field-independent people. This strategy may be advantageous in some situations because people who are sensitive to social cues will be more socially aware. However, the same style may be a disadvantage in situations where attending to others may be distracting and inappropriate (for example, looking at pedestrians rather than concentrating on steering between obstacles when driving).

Reliance on internal or external cues can also result in individual differences in attributional judgements about the causes of events. For example, some people prefer to attribute their performance on a task to their own effort whereas others prefer to attribute their performance to external factors beyond their control. Rotter (1966) described two cognitive styles which people use in evaluating the causes of their performance: while some people adopt an internal locus of control, preferring to attribute their performance to themselves, others prefer an external locus of control, in which they attribute their performance to external factors.

Thinking styles on cognitive tasks

Impulsive cognitive styles

Kagan (1965) has proposed a further cognitive style to account for individual differences in performance on specific cognitive tasks in which several alternative options are available, but there is uncertainty as to which option is correct. Kagan suggests that on such tasks people may adopt either a rapid information processing style, or a more deliberate style, in which decisions are taken more slowly. He therefore called this cognitive style **reflection-impulsivity**. To test his ideas, Kagan devised the Matching Familiar Figures Test (or MFFT). In this, children are presented with a number of figures which differ from each other in one or more details. The children are then asked to select from these figures the one which exactly matches a target example. Kagan found that children's responses on the MFFT could be placed in four categories: thus children could be classified as either fast and accurate, fast and inaccurate, slow and accurate or slow and inaccurate. According to Kagan, fast inaccurate children are using an impulsive cognitive style whereas slow accurate children are using a reflective cognitive style. In other words, Kagan assumed that impulsive behaviour on the MFFT is best explained by the use of a particular kind of thinking style (a fast approach which leads to many errors). The question remains, however, as to whether the thinking styles of fast accurate children on the MFFT can be distinguished in some way from those of slow accurate children. Unfortunately, so far, research has been unable to describe the different cognitive styles or strategies which children in these groups may use. This has led some critics to argue that as fast accurate children and slow accurate children cannot be distinguished in terms of their thinking styles, the fast accurate children may simply be more 'intelligent' (i.e. they may differ on a personality trait).

More recent research by Dickman (1990), however, has suggested that there may be two sorts of impulsive cognitive style, each related to different behavioural consequences in social situations; these are functional impulsivity and dysfunctional impulsivity. Dickman agrees with Kagan that some individuals adopt a rapid approach to information processing. However, he found that whereas some individuals may sacrifice errors for speed on cognitive tasks, these same people tend to benefit from their impulsive behaviour in social situations (their impulsive style is therefore functional). Dickman therefore suggests that a functional impulsive cognitive style based on rapid information processing may have different consequences for cognitive performance than performance in social situations. Thus, whereas the tendency to think quickly may result in many errors on a cognitive task, it may be beneficial in social situations because someone who is able to think quickly will be able to take advantage of social opportunities.

On the other hand, Dickman found that other individuals who report that they tend to behave impulsively in social situations with negative consequences appear to adopt a relatively slow response style on cognitive figure matching tasks; Dickman called this style 'dysfunctional impulsivity'. Individuals who adopt a dysfunctional style appear not to consider social situations carefully and thus get into trouble and frequently regret their actions, yet their performance on cognitive tasks is deliberate and relatively error free. Further research by Brunas-Wagstaff *et al.* (1994), however, suggests that dysfunctional impulsivity may be related to difficulties in selecting amongst many competing alternative responses on cognitive tasks. This tendency appears not to be related to a rapid processing strategy. Their results suggest that dysfunctionals do make errors on cognitive tasks which involve an element of interference, even though they adopt a relatively slow and deliberate style. One implication of this finding is that a dysfunctional cognitive style may have negative consequences in any situation where the options available are numerous and indistinct.

General theories of cognitive style

Kagan's theory of reflection-impulsivity focuses on the styles adopted by children to process information under very specific conditions. Other cognitive psychologists, however, have attempted to construct more general theories which aim to describe global cognitive styles which distinguish between individuals, rather than to identify specific styles associated with relatively specific contexts. These theories therefore are almost indistinguishable from personality theories, because they predict that individual differences in cognition may have general consequences for people's behaviour in a variety of situations. For instance, according to Gregorc (1985), people can be categorised according to four cognitive styles based on two information processing dimensions. The first dimension, concrete versus abstract processing, refers to the extent to which individuals attend to the physical and observable or to the conceptual, non-concrete characteristics of any situation. The second dimension, random versus sequential, refers to the tendency to either order events in sequence (step by step) or in a web-like manner. Thus, an individual may be a concrete-random processor, or a concrete-sequential processor, an abstract-random or an abstract-sequential processor.

Sternberg (1988) further proposed a novel theory of cognitive style based on the various functions, levels and forms of government. According to Sternberg, people organise their societies in ways which reflect systems of organisation internal to the mind. Thus, the functions, levels and forms of government represent styles of mental self-government, or cognitive styles which people adopt for the organisation of information. Three main functions of government are the legislative (which involves creating, formulating and planning); the executive (whose function is to maintain structure, procedure and rules) and the judicial (whose function is to evaluate and question). Thus, individuals may function predominantly by adopting strategies which favour creativity, formulating and planning (a legislative person); organising according to procedures and rules (an executive person); or questioning and evaluating evidence (a judicial person). The two levels of government are the local and global levels. Individuals may focus on specific or concrete details (as does local government) or prefer projects involving all-encompassing or abstract ideas (represented by the global level). Finally, the four forms of government: the monarchic, anarchic, hierarchic and oligarchic, reflect the following individual strategies: focusing fully on one aspect of a task and seeing it through to its conclusion (monarchic); showing a flexible approach to problem-solving (anarchic); creating priorities and dealing with each in order (hierarchic); and setting multiple goals, that are equally important (oligarchic).

Cognitive styles in applied psychology

Although there is a large body of research into cognitive styles, it is in the area of **applied psychology** that cognitive styles have come into their own, and many applied psychologists have used cognitive styles as the theoretical basis for a variety of applied models of behaviour and behavioural change.

Psychopathology and attributional styles

One area of applied clinical psychology in which thinking styles based on the socio-cognitive research on attribution have been particularly useful is in the understanding of clinical depression.

Thus, Abramson *et al.* (1978) have suggested that depressed patients may be distinguished from people who are not suffering from symptoms of depression on the basis of their attributions of causality for negative events. Attributional style is assessed using the Attributional Style Questionnaire (or ASQ), which asks subjects to evaluate the causes of various hypothetical life events, including positive life events (such as being promoted in a career) and negative life events (such as job loss or the break-up of a relationship). Three dimensions are then used to establish the nature of attributions of causality. These are whether the person makes mostly internal or external attributions (whether they tend to blame themselves, or some external factor); whether their attributions are stable or unstable (whether the cause of the event is seen as a one-off, transient cause, or a permanent problem); and whether the attribution is global (applies to many situations in the person's life) or specific (applies to just one or a few situations). So, for example, a person may perceive the cause of a failed relationship to be his or her own fault (an internal attribution) or due to circumstances, such as the pressures on the relationship of having to live apart while one of the partners was working away from home (an external attribution). In either case, the cause may be perceived as stable or unstable. Thus an internal attribution can have a stable cause which is unchanging (such as: 'I am not worthy of my partner's love') or an unstable cause (such as: 'I had an extra-marital affair'). Similarly, an external attribution may have a stable cause (such as: 'I will always have to work away from home, I have no choice') or unstable (such as: 'I was only working away on this one occasion; I can change my job'). Finally, the causes of an event may be viewed as specific (such as: 'only this relationship has failed for this reason') or global (such as: 'all my relationships fail for the same reason').

According to Abramson *et al.*, while non-depressed subjects tend to attribute the causes of negative events to outside factors, and positive events to internal causes, in line with the self-serving bias (see Chapter 6), depressed patients tend to make attributional judgements for negative events which are internal, stable and global. In other words, when bad things happen, depressed

111

individuals are likely to blame themselves, to assume that they can do nothing to change whatever it is about themselves which is the cause of the problem and, furthermore, to feel responsible for failures in many areas of their lives. Abramson *et al.* therefore assume that depressed people exhibit a tendency to mis-attribute the causes of negative life events and thus to blame themselves for bad things which happen to them.

However, other clinical psychologists have criticised this model for a number of reasons. First, whereas the model assumes that a major factor in the thinking of depressed subjects is self-blame, self-blame may not be a feature of all types of depression, and it has been suggested that self-blame may only be evident in some sub-groups of depressed patients. Moreover, the pattern of responses shown by depressed patients on the Attributional Style Questionnaire may not represent a tendency to mis-attribute the causes of negative events; rather perhaps it is non-depressed 'normal' subjects who exhibit biased attributions of causality. Maybe the attributions of depressed patients are actually more realistic. Also, some clinical psychologists have argued that responses on the ASQ may change with the onset of depressive symptoms, thus casting doubt over the validity of the ASQ as a tool capable of predicting the onset of depression (Brewin, 1988).

Other researchers have suggested that attributional styles may be relevant to the problems of paranoia and delusions in clinical patients. For instance, Kaney and Bentall (1989) found that patients with persecutory delusions gave abnormally external, specific and global attributions for negative events on the ASQ, whereas they gave abnormally internal, specific and global attributions for positive events. In other words, delusional subjects appeared to show an extreme version of the self-serving bias in their attributional judgements. Bentall has argued that this cognitive bias may represent a self-protective mechanism. Most individuals, in operating a self-serving bias for attributions of success and failure, are able to maintain their self-esteem because they can take the credit for good outcomes and not blame themselves too much for bad outcomes. In deluded patients, however, this self-esteem enhancing strategy is exaggerated, so that the man who exhibits symptoms of paranoia is convinced that when bad things happen he is being persecuted by external agents. Also, as he is only able to trust his own judgement (because others may be persecuting him), he may manifest an exaggerated belief in his own importance in causing good events.

The differences in responses on the ASQ observed between normal subjects and depressed and deluded patients suggest that individual differences in preferences for thinking about events and their causes appear to be associated with at least some psychopathologies. This approach to applied clinical psychology therefore involves trying to alter the ways in which people think about their circumstances, rather than intervening to alter their physiology or their environment. Such an approach may be more practical, as it may not always be possible to establish underlying physiological or environmental causes of psychopathology with any degree of certainty.

Learning styles

In the area of educational psychology, research on cognitive styles has been applied to an understanding of how students learn. Thus, Renzulli and Smith (1978) have suggested that individuals adopt various learning styles, each of which may be perceived as appropriate for different methods of teaching. Research on academic performance in higher education has also indicated that differences in performance between students may be related to differences in the process of learning. In other words, differences in student performance may reflect different learning styles which students bring to bear on various educational tasks. For example, Svensson (1977) distinguished between holistic and atomistic approaches in the analysis of text (such as when reading course-relevant materials). Holistic learners tended to consider the text as a means of grasping concepts which were beyond or were underlying the text (such as author's intention, main points, conclusions to be drawn), whereas atomistic learners tended to focus on the text itself; they attempted to memorise sections rather than achieve an overall understanding. Similar strategies were identified by Marton and Saljo (1976) who used the terms 'deep' and 'surface' processors. Marton and Saljo found a relationship between level of processing adopted by students (whether they focused on surface aspects or whether they tried to extract 'deeper' underlying concepts and meaning) and students' assessed performance. Whereas the majority of deep processors achieved performance outcomes in the 'A' or 'B' grade categories, surface processors tended to achieve lower 'C' or 'D' grades. However, the precise psychological variables which may underlie observed differences in learning styles remain to be defined, though Marton *et al.* (1984) suggest that deep and surface processors may differ in such areas as their attention to detail, perceptions of time pressure and 'cognitive projects' (what the learner is trying to accomplish) as well as on personality variables such as anxiety or motivation.

Other researchers have described individual differences in students' approaches to essay writing. For example, Norton *et al.* (1996) found that students in higher education appear to have their own expectancies about what it is that their tutors require of a good essay and that students adopt a variety of strategies to help them to achieve a good grade. Students' actual performance on their essays appeared to depend on whether the students adopted strategies that were consistent with the requirements of tutors. However, even more important were the strategies which students used to help them 'spot' what it was that tutors expected of them. For instance, whereas some students tried to pick up clues, or hints given by tutors in class (a cue-conscious strategy) or actively sought out information about how to write a good essay from tutors (a cue-seeking strategy), other students appeared to believe that hard work was enough on its own to achieve a good grade (as these students had no particular strategy, they have been described as 'cue-deaf') (Miller and Parlett, 1974). Norton and Crowley (1995) also found that students can be taught to adopt alternative (more appropriate) learning strategies for writing essays and revising for exams if these are communicated to them directly as part of their course, suggesting that individual differences in students' performance in Higher Education may reflect different learning styles more than ability or temperament.

Other approaches to individual differences in learning styles have focused on the more general cognitive styles of reflection-impulsivity (Kagan, 1965) and field independence–dependence as predictors of effective learning in adult students and school-children. For example, in a study of adult students learning English as a foreign language, Jamieson (1992) found that a rapid, error free information processing style and a tendency to be field independent were related to superior performance on a test of English proficiency. Reflective students who adopted a fast-accurate style on Kagan's Matching Familiar Figures Test gained higher language proficiency scores than students who adopted alternative styles of response; and students who were field independent (measured on the embedded figures test, a cognitive measure of the field dependence–independence construct) were also found to score higher than field-dependent students on a test of language proficiency. In schoolchildren also, the cognitive style of reflection-impulsivity has been related to school performance. Messer (1970) found that an impulsive style was related to school failure, and Hall and Russell (1974) found that an impulsive style was associated with reading difficulties in children.

Whatever underlies differences in information processing, research into cognitive styles in an educational context suggests that people may approach the educational tasks set for them in very different ways, with different consequences for educational success. Identifying students' preferred styles of learning across different educational contexts may thus prove to be a useful starting point in helping under-achievers to adopt more appropriate learning strategies (those which high achievers appear to employ automatically). This approach has the advantage of treating student learners as people who are approaching educational tasks in the wrong way and who therefore need pointing in the right direction, rather than labelling students according to their position on trait dimensions of ability, such as 'intelligent–unintelligent'.

Criminal thinking styles

Various psychologists studying crime and deviance have formulated theories which suggest that specific cognitive styles may be used by criminals to process crime-relevant information. For example, criminality has been associated with an impulsive cognitive thinking style (Ross and Fabiano, 1985) whereby criminals fail to stop and think before acting; with an external locus of control (Beck and Ollendick, 1976; Kumchy and Sayer, 1980) whereby criminals explain their behaviour as being caused by external rather than internal factors; and with poor social problem-solving skills or a reduced ability to attend to social cues based on an inability to see things from another person's perspective (Freedman *et al.* 1978; Chandler, 1973). (See Hollin, 1989 for a review of cognitive approaches to crime.)

One of the most comprehensive cognitive theories of criminality, however, is that of Yochelson and Samenow (1976). The theory of criminality proposed by Yochelson and Samenow is based mostly on qualitative data involving interviews with male offenders attending a psychiatric hospital. On the basis of these interviews, Yochelson and Samenow have concluded that criminals exhibit a number of preferred styles and errors of thinking which define the criminal mind. They suggest upwards of fifty of these styles and errors. However, the most important characteristics of criminal thinking can be categorised according to the following three general areas: emotionality, sentimentality and criminal ideas.

Emotionality According to Yochelson and Samenow, criminals are characterised by fear, an emotion which underlies much of what the criminal thinks and does. In particular, fear of humiliation and 'put-downs'. This gives rise to a number of compensatory thought patterns or a set of cognitive coping mechanisms: the criminal strives to maintain 'machismo' or 'toughness' (a fiercely masculine self-image), which involves showing aggression in anticipation of any potential threat to self-esteem and maintaining physical superiority (keeping in good physical shape) and social and material superiority (demonstrated through sexual conquests and material possessions). The need to maintain 'toughness' or 'machismo' dominates much of the criminal's thinking, and he therefore develops mental strategies associated with maintaining this image which distinguish his thinking from that of the general population.

Sentimentality   In contrast to the tough image which the criminal seeks to cultivate, he is also characterised by a set of emotions directed towards the helpless or disadvantaged in society (for example, children, the elderly, animals). In particular, criminals also display an unusual degree of sentimentality towards the family, especially their own mothers. As this sentimental side would appear to be inconsistent with the maintenance of a tough image, the criminal accommodates these two sides by developing a set of cognitions which enable him to 'fragment' or separate thoughts associated with machismo from thoughts associated with sentimentality. This enables the criminal to separate moral thoughts from moral behaviour, so that he can reconcile some of his criminal activities (stealing from an elderly person, for example) with his attitudes (sentimentality about the elderly).

Criminal ideas   Finally, the criminals studied by Yochelson and Samenow appeared to show an obsession with seeking criminal opportunities and with planning and fantasising about criminal activities, so that thoughts about crime were almost an addiction. Thus, the criminal will attend to situations and opportunities which present themselves which most people would fail to notice (for instance, in a busy street full of people, most people would not be aware of someone's purse showing in the pocket of their overcoat, whereas the criminal would tune into this cue).

According to Yochelson and Samenow, therefore, criminals can be distinguished by a characteristic set of cognitions or thinking patterns the combined use of which mean that the criminal is completely lacking in any insight into the immorality of his way of life. In fact, according to Yochelson and Samenow as the criminal believes that fundamentally he is a good person, who just happens to have broken the law, the first step in getting the criminal to alter his behaviour is to make him aware of his deviant cognitive styles, so that he can work at changing his thinking patterns and ultimately his behaviour.

Cognitive styles or personality traits?

Theories of cognitive style therefore focus on the information processing strategies which individuals prefer to use in a variety of contexts. However, some cognitive styles may be difficult to distinguish from personality traits, especially where these styles make general predictions with regard to behaviour across many situations. The theories proposed by Gregorc and Sternberg, for instance, suggest that people may be characterised by certain cognitive styles which may have general consequences for their behaviour in most situations. On the other hand, according to Kagan, the style of reflection-impulsivity is only described in terms of performance on a specific task: the MFFT. Nevertheless, one could argue that a person who consistently adopts an impulsive rather than a reflective style of information processing possesses an impulsive personality. Moreover, Yochelson and Samenow's description of criminal thinking styles could equally be considered to reflect a criminal personality.

One major difficulty for researchers of cognitive styles, however, has been that their studies have tended to be descriptive rather than explanatory. In other words, although their research has described many of the strategies which people use when faced with a variety of different problems to solve, these descriptions do not tell us why people employ different strategies, or where those strategies come from in the first place. Some cognitive psychologists have therefore proposed a theoretical framework to explain how people's thinking styles might be organised and controlled around goals for future action.

Summary

In this chapter, individual differences in cognitive styles (preferred ways of using abilities or thinking processes) have been examined in relation to a number of theoretical and applied areas of psychology. It seems that cognitive styles may represent a particularly useful approach to the study of individual differences within applied psychology, because they relate to behaviour in specific contexts, whereas personality traits require extensive measurement over time, and across a variety of contexts. Nevertheless when an individual consistently adheres to a particular cognitive style, it could be argued that there is little to distinguish between a cognitive style and a personality trait. For instance, it seems reasonable to say that someone who adopts a consistently impulsive response style, across many situations, has an impulsive personality.

Further reading

See end of Chapter 8.

Chapter 8

Thinking styles and personal goals

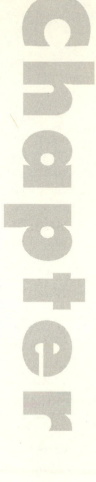

S O FAR, IT HAS BEEN SUGGESTED that cognitive styles may represent an alternative to the idea of temperaments when it comes to accounting for individual differences. However, the assumption that cognitive styles may underlie differences in behaviour presents the psychologist with a new set of problems. In particular, it is not clear why individuals appear to favour different cognitive styles or strategies in the same situations. One possibility is that different individuals use different strategies to achieve different outcomes. In other words, individuals may choose a strategy which they believe to be consistent with achieving their individual **goals**. According to Monsell (1996), both cognition and behaviour may be determined by and organised around goals for future action. Goals are therefore seen as activity energisers which determine both our thoughts and actions. Monsell (1996), suggests the following possible hierarchical organisation for some of the goals which may energise human thoughts and actions: at the top of the hierarchy are fundamental and abstract goals, like survival of the species and reproduction. Goals in the middle of the hierarchy may be part biological and part cultural; such as access to food, shelter, social acceptability, social success, dominance, comfort, knowledge of the world, sex, companionship and co-operation. These broad goals have time spans of many years. Further down the hierarchy again are goals which span days, such as reading a book; or hours, such as painting a ceiling; or minutes, such as making a cup of tea; or even fractions of seconds, such as recognising a word.

If our behaviour is indeed directed towards and organised around goals, then it is necessary to explain how goals might be established, how they are maintained and how they mediate behaviour. Although it is not yet clear exactly how goals serve to organise our thoughts and actions, recent research in cognitive psychology and in developmental psychology has provided some interesting insights.

Establishing and maintaining goals

Establishing goals and forming intentions

According to Ajzen (1988), we may establish particular goals for future action via 'intention'. Forming an intention involves integrating several kinds of information which lead to the formation of an 'attitude', a 'subjective norm' for action and 'perceived behavioural control'. Our analysis of the information then increases or decreases the probability of carrying out an action. Thus, first we consider the outcomes an action will produce and how much we personally want those outcomes, to form an 'attitude'. Attitudes are therefore personal orientations to the act being considered. Then we consider whether other people close to us would approve of the action and how much their opinion of us really matters to us. This establishes a 'subjective norm' for the behaviour. Finally, we evaluate how easy or hard it will be for us to carry out the behaviour (this is perceived behavioural control). Thereafter, all we have to do is to weigh up the three elements, attitude, subjective norm and perceived behavioural control, to determine an intention to act. For example, in forming an intention to leave a current relationship, a person may form his own attitude towards leaving, consider that of his friends and family to the break-up of the relationship, and finally, consider whether he feels able to leave (can he tell his partner it is over? Can he cope with the financial consequences?). Once he has formed an intention for action, he has established a goal for future action.

Azjen's model, however, assumes that the process of establishing goals via intention is quite deliberate. Other approaches suggest that goals may emerge in a more automatic and abstract way from our analysis of situations and that behaviour is not planned, rather it emerges in a passive way from activation of information held in memory. In support of this view, researchers often refer to cognitive studies of priming which show that information activated in one situation can influence behaviour in another situation, apparently without the subject being aware of the influence. For example, Carver and Scheier (1992) describe two studies: one on priming which showed that the reactions of male students towards an attractive female were influenced by prior exposure to a story involving a boy-meets-girl situation; and another which showed that subjects who were exposed to hostile word sets gave more shocks to a learner in a subsequent trial. In both these situations, it seems that people's behaviour was 'primed' by exposure to recent information which was readily available and therefore easily applied to behaviour which followed. This approach suggests that people have abstract schemas for action stored in memory which can be triggered by situations. For example, we may activate a schema which directs our behaviour appropriately when we enter a church (we walk slowly, speak quietly, etc.) because the situation triggers this appropriate sequence of action directly, without any effort or intention on our part, just as we might form an association to an object (such as when 'chair' activates 'table'). Schank and Abelson (1977) propose that we use 'scripts' to understand events and guide behaviour. For all familiar situations, we have a script which reminds us of how we are supposed to behave. For example, we may have a script for behaviour in a supermarket, on a date, taking the children to school and so on. Such scripts are assumed to be automatically activated rather than actively constructed on the spot, so that the process of setting behavioural goals within situations is assumed to be implicit, not the result of reasoning or information processing as suggested by Azjen.

Maintaining goals: the role of feedback

However goals may be established, once a goal has been set (an intention formed, or a schema activated) the goal must be maintained for as long as is necessary to attain it. In other words, we must have a mechanism for comparing the present state to the goal state, so that we know how far away we are from attaining our goal, and we must continue to plan and control our thoughts and actions until this end is achieved. In comparing our present state to the goal state we therefore need a standard for comparison and a mechanism for self-regulation which feeds back to us information about whether we are meeting that standard.

Many goals involve setting standards which are quite neutral and merely represent a desired end state such as the goal of getting in a video and a take-away for next Saturday night. Other goals, however, involve evaluative standards, or standards of excellence. For example, the goal of being able to complete the London Marathon involves evaluating one's fitness at various stages, and comparing one's present condition with the desired state or standard required to make the goal a reality. In each case, the process of comparing where you are now, with where you want to be, may be rather different. In the first case, you need only make sure that your behaviour is directed towards your goal, or kept on track. Occasionally, you may need to check yourself, for example, if you set out to the video rental store, but you forget your purse. In the second case, you must not only monitor your behaviour to keep yourself on the right track towards your goal (such as making sure you train every day, acquire the entry form, fill it in, etc.), but you must also evaluate your fitness with a standard of excellence in mind (an ideal level of fitness which you have set for yourself). There is evidence to suggest a process of self-regulation and feedback does operate in directing human behaviour towards goals. For instance it is well-established that people who are given knowledge of the results achieved on a task are able to benefit more than people who are not given any feedback about their performance. When people know that their performance on previous trials was poor, they tend to try harder on future trials. On the other hand, people who are told that their performance meets with the standard, or goal, tend to set themselves higher goals, or level off their performance (Carver and Scheier, 1992).

However, some psychologists have argued that although it seems likely that people do organise and maintain control over behaviour in this way, the model is too simple (see Carver and Scheier, 1992) because human behaviour is highly complex and it needs to be flexible. This has led to the proposal that feedback mechanisms which organise behaviour are themselves organised into chains of connecting feedback loops called a 'decision tree'. This allows us to adjust our response when we encounter an outcome that is unexpected. For instance, if our goal is to photocopy some documents but we go over to the photocopier and the copier is out of order, we can automatically trigger a new goal, and new action schemas, to deal with this unexpected change to our plans. Another approach is to assume that feedback mechanisms may be arranged into hierarchies. Here the assumption is that interconnections between feedback loops are organised according to superordinate and subordinate goals, with the subordinate goals providing guides for action. Thus, if one superordinate goal is to graduate from college, this would be associated with a number of sub-goals designed to achieve this end, from applying to colleges, studying to pass the entrance exam, or physical goals associated with controlling movement, such as lifting a pen and moving the hand to fill out the application form.

Another criticism of the concept of feedback mechanisms in maintaining behaviour is that the model is too mechanistic and does not take any account of human characteristics such as emotion and its influence on planning and working towards goals. However, Simon (1967) has argued that emotions are not incompatible with an information processing model of self-regulation. Instead, he has proposed that emotions may be signals to re-prioritise our goal-directed behaviour. Thus, anxiety is a signal that we are pursuing the wrong goals (for example seeking promotion at work) when we should be directing our efforts towards other more important goals which we have neglected (such as taking care of our health or family).

Slips of action

Another way of approaching the issue of how goals are maintained and how behaviour is organised in accordance with goals or plans of action is to look at instances in which behaviour has become disrupted. By investigating those occasions on which goals fail to be maintained, we can thus gain clues as to how goal-maintenance is normally achieved.

Studies of control failures in normal cognition suggest that slips of action in everyday life can reveal much about the way in which behaviour is normally organised. Some slips of action appear to reflect a failure to control behaviour, as when our intention to carry out some action is interrupted and we carry out an unintended behaviour instead (for example, setting out in the car in the wrong direction for our intended destination), or when we perform behaviours in the wrong sequence (putting on your shoes before your socks). Slips of action of this kind can be contrasted with more straightforward errors of recognition, such as picking up a neighbour's wineglass at a dinner table, because they suggest that something has gone wrong with our system for organising behaviour around goals, whereas errors of recognition are merely errors of perception (Monsell, 1996). Investigations of action errors have helped to understand the causes of these errors. For example, Norman (1981) and Reason (1990) asked people to keep diaries of everyday slips of action and found that errors can be categorised into seven main types (see Monsell, 1996). These are:

- capture errors, where stronger habits appear to take over almost automatically, as in setting off in the wrong direction along a more familiar route
- cross-talk errors, where two plans of action become confused, or get swopped over, such as putting the pan in the fridge and the milk in the pan cupboard
- lost intentions and failed triggers, for example when you find yourself walking into the bedroom, but you've forgotten why you are there
- detached intentions, such as intending to open the window, but opening the door instead
- 'Program counter failures', when you lose count of the steps needed to complete a sequence (such as forgetting whether you have put one or two sugars into the cup of coffee)
- dissociations between formulation and execution of intentions, where you fail to respond to an altered plan of action, such as being asked to leave the cutlery out of the draw, but continuing to put it away
- errors resulting from overintrusive control/monitoring, like concentrating too hard on the movements required to hit

the ball in a tennis game, and thereby failing to focus attention on where the ball actually is.

An analysis of these sorts of errors suggests a number of things about how we control and maintain behaviour. One common theme is that more frequent or recent behaviours usually take over from less recent or infrequent behaviours when an action sequence is interrupted. In other words, the better practised a task, the more likely it is to intrude. A second observation is that well-practised acts can apparently be unintentionally triggered, or at least a person can be unaware of forming an intention to initiate the behaviour. Such evidence therefore appears to support the view that behavioural maintenance and control are relatively automatic.

Other studies have examined failures of control resulting from brain damage. These studies suggest that people who have damage to the frontal lobes of the brain exhibit specific impairments in the programming, initiation, regulation and monitoring of mental and behavioural activity. Such individuals exhibit behavioural symptoms such as perseveration (whereby a person goes on performing some simple action inappropriately, like washing the same plate over and over again) or they may fail to initiate behaviour spontaneously, though they are capable of repeating actions. For example, they may fail to initiate speech, but can repeat words. Another characteristic of patients with frontal lobe damage is that they are distractible: that is, they appear unable to maintain sustained focused attention. These clinical studies suggest that the control of mental processes and behavioural sequences may have a physiological basis in frontal lobe functioning, which is disrupted in patients with frontal lobe damage.

The development of goal-directed behaviour in children

One final approach to understanding how goals may be established and maintained is to trace the development of goal-directed behaviour in childhood. Developmental studies of behavioural control suggest that initially children do not possess the ability to regulate their own behaviour. Instead, they must rely on adults to control their behaviour. For example, young infants cannot calm themselves when they are upset, and must rely on their parents to soothe them (Schaffer, 1996). Kopp (1982) has described a number of developmental stages in which children appear to gradually acquire increasing amounts of control over their own behaviour. According to Kopp during the first 2–3 months of life, infants posses only very basic strategies for controlling their behaviour, for example they may use comfort sucking to soothe them when they feel upset, but mostly they must rely on comfort provided externally by the carer. Between 3 and 9 months the infant develops control over its behaviour in relation to objects, such as in reaching or grasping for a toy. However, this appears to occur as an automatic response to the presence of the object, rather than following a conscious or deliberate plan. Only in the first year of life does behavioural control become truly deliberate. At this age, the child becomes increasingly able to obey external commands (initially these commands involve physical signals, such as turning a child away from something, rather than verbal commands), however it does not regulate its own behaviour in the absence of the carer. From about 2 years onwards, children become capable of obeying adult requests even in the adult's absence but it is not until about 3 years of age that the child can regulate its own behaviour by choosing to comply or not comply with directives. At this stage, children are truly able to regulate their behaviour because for the first time they appear to show evidence of deliberate non-compliance. Children at this stage begin to develop strategies and social skills which enable them to express their autonomy. Kuczynski and Kochanska (1990) have identified some of the strategies which children use to avoid complying with adult directives. These include ignoring the request or directive; refusing to comply by saying 'no' or shaking the head; physical refusal, such as pushing the parent away, or throwing an object on the ground; using excuses ('I'm too little'); bargaining ('I'll do it if I can have a cookie') and negotiating (a combination of bargaining and excuses).

The child's progression from an infant lacking in behavioural control, to a little individual, able to employ strategies which help it to plan courses of action (involving compliance or defiance) appears to parallel cognitive, social and biological processes which govern development. According to Kagan (1981), children around two-and-a-half years old begin to notice flaws in objects for the first time (such as a crack in a cup, or a teddy without an arm). Kagan suggests that the emergence of this ability may indicate that the child has internalised a standard for physical objects, and is able to compare objects to that standard. With the growth of language skills, the child can discuss its standards with other children and adults. Standards understood initially in relation to objects soon become evident in relation to social behaviour (so that the child can distinguish something as being 'strange' or 'funny', and eventually also something 'bad' or 'good'). According to Schaffer (1996), the rules which define standards are learned within the context of family routines, but the child must have attained a level of cognitive maturity before it can assimilate the information necessary to abstract these rules, based on biologically determined maturation.

Turiel (1983) further distinguishes between two sorts of standards which children acquire: the first type of standard is based on rules for comparing behaviour with arbitrary conventions (we have tea at 6 o'clock), though in time the child may learn that the rule is not fixed (we could have tea at 6 or 7). The second type of standard is based on rules for comparing behaviour with moral conventions (I must not hit my brother). With this type of standard for behaviour, the child must learn that it is universal, and should apply no matter what the context. According to Turiel, the child therefore develops standards of behaviour by comparing the conventions within its family to those conventions which appear to operate outside the family. In this way it establishes standards for behaviour which may be loosely defined (in the case of arbitrary conventions) or rigidly defined (such as moral conventions). Hereafter, the child may set goals which are aimed at achieving those standards, and it may organise its behaviour and thought processes towards achieving those standards.

Behavioural control therefore seems to develop through a process of stages, and children at later stages become both progressively more able to organise their behaviour in a goal-directed way, and to make use of a variety of strategies for attaining their goals. This variety in the strategies used by even very young children appears to represent the earliest evidence of individual differences in cognitive styles organised according to individual goals. Initially the only two goals available to the child are compliance or non-compliance with adult directives, however, as the child grows up, the number of possible goals may increase considerably, as do the number of possible strategies for reaching the goals.

Summary

Research on intentions, goal-maintenance and feedback, slips of action and developmental studies of the acquisition of goal-directed behaviour in children suggests that much of human thought and action may be organised around goals. Individuals' preferred strategies for dealing with many situations may therefore have a basis in the goals which they set themselves and aspire to. Some of these goals may be fundamental and abstract, such as biological goals that concern the survival of the species, whereas others may be social goals such as getting promoted at work. The psychological evidence tends to suggest that many of these goals may be established and maintained in a relatively automatic way without our awareness, and goals may thus serve to energise behaviour in an implicit rather than an explicit way. Finally, as different people may have different goals, many individual differences in behaviour and thought may be explained in terms of goal differences rather than differences in temperament or personality.

Further reading (Chapters 7 and 8)

Carver, C.S. and Scheier, M.F. (1992). 2nd edn. *Perspectives on Personality*. Allyn & Bacon. Chapter 16: Contemporary cognitive views.

Chapter 17: Self-regulation. A good overview of the concept of goals as determinants of behaviour in individual differences psychology.

McAdams, D.P. (1994). 2nd edn. *The Person: An Introduction to Personality Psychology*. Harcourt Brace. Chapter 9: Cognitive approaches to the person. A good chapter on the cognitive approach to personality and individual differences.

Mischel, W. (1993). 5th edn. *Introduction to Personality*. Harcourt Brace. Chapter 15: Encoding, constructs and expectancies. Chapter 16: Self-regulatory strategies and competencies. Mischel's approach marries the cognitive and social-learning perspectives on personality, in these easy to read chapters.

Personality, temperament and thought

O N FIRST CONSIDERATION, the personality and cognitive style approaches to the study of individual differences would seem to present radically different positions. The personality approach assumes that individuals possess dispositions or tendencies to respond to situations in a consistent way, and that their behaviour will therefore be relatively consistent across situations. Thus, for example, a Freudian anal personality will exhibit anal characteristics regardless of the context in which his or her behaviour is recorded, and an extrovert will be more outgoing and sociable than an introvert, in many different circumstances. However, the situationists have argued that behaviour is very much determined by situations. Recognising, therefore, that behaviour can be inconsistent across situations, personality theorists have come up with a compromise solution: the interactionist perspective. This suggests that behaviour in any particular situation is determined by both dispositional and situational causes. However, such an approach does not improve our ability to predict how a particular person will behave in a number of different circumstances. Moreover, it cannot predict precisely when behaviour is likely to be consistent, and when it is likely to be inconsistent. This means that we cannot even draw conclusions about how different people are likely to behave in a specific situation, because we do not know whether their dispositions or the situation are most likely to determine their behaviour in the particular context.

In order to understand when a person will behave in a particular way, in a particular situation, it may therefore be better to try and determine how different people perceive and think about the same situation. This is the **cognitive style** approach. However, although cognitive psychologists are able to tell us something about the processes involved in evaluating different situations, and the different ways in which people make use of those processes (their strategies or cognitive styles), they cannot tell us exactly when a particular strategy will be used by a particular individual. One way forward is to assume that cognitions (thought processes) and behaviour are both organised around goals for future action. Thus, instead of assuming that behaviour is determined by something called 'personality' which resides within us, this approach would suggest that behaviour is energised by plans of action, or goals. Some of these goals may be very basic goals to do with survival of the species (finding enough to eat, finding a sexual partner) whereas others may be social goals (like getting a promotion at work). If we can define people's goals in different situations, we should be able to work out the behaviours and cognitive strategies which individuals are most likely to adopt to maximise their chances of goal attainment. This approach has an important advantage over dispositional theories because behaviour which is determined by goals need not necessarily be consistent across situations, because each situation may offer different possibilities for goal attainment. On the other hand, perhaps the main disadvantage of this approach is that it assumes that human reasoning is a systematic process, whereas studies of social cognition suggest that our thinking is not always very systematic.

However, instead of trying to establish which approach is the best approach to the study of individual differences, perhaps it might be more fruitful to suggest that when psychologists talk about goals and dispositions, they may be talking about the same things in a slightly different way.

Personality traits as goal-based categories

Let us reconsider some of the dispositional or personality approaches to individual differences. According to psychoanalytic psychologists like Freud, human behaviour is determined by sexual and aggressive instincts and human beings constantly strive to seek ways of expressing these instincts in a socially acceptable way. According to phenomenological psychologists such as

Maslow and Rogers, behaviour is driven by a motive for self-enhancement or a self-actualising tendency. For Eysenck, people behave in different ways according to whether they seek stimulation (extroverts) or avoid stimulation (introverts). Finally, according to social-learning theorists, behaviour is determined by our expectations of obtaining reinforcement or punishment. However, any of these explanations for behaviour from within personality psychology could be described in terms of goals for future action. For instance, it could be argued that according to Freud, our main goal is to express our sexual or aggressive instincts in a socially acceptable way. For Eysenck, the goal is to maximise our chances of either obtaining or avoiding stimulation depending on our physiologically determined needs; thus an extrovert will seek company and excitement to maximise his chances of stimulation, whereas an introvert will avoid company and excitement, to maximise his chances of avoiding stimulation. According to Bandura, the goal could be seen as maximising our chances of reinforcement and minimising punishment, and according to Maslow the goal might be to satisfy basic needs arranged in a hierarchical order of importance, so that the ultimate goal of self-actualisation can be achieved. However, it may be the case that not all of the characteristics we associate with personality are goal based.

What is the relationship between personality traits and goals?

One of the main problems associated with predicting behaviour from a knowledge of people's personality traits or dispositions is deciding which behaviours should hang together under a particular trait. The problem of deciding which behaviours belong together, and which do not, really comes down to a cognitive decision about which members of a particular category are most typical. According to cognitive psychologists, one basis of judgements of typicality is that of physical similarity or family resemblance. Thus, the category 'bird' may be defined in terms of a prototype or best example of members belonging to that category. A typical bird is quite small, has feathers, a beak and flies. We can then evaluate objects according to how closely they fit this prototype. Using this system of categorisation, a robin is a typical example of a bird (it is small, has wings, a beak and flies) whereas an ostrich is not a typical bird (it does have feathers, a beak and small wings, but it does not fly and is large). This type of categorisation is called a taxonomic category. On the other hand, we may use goal-derived categories to decide how the members of a category should be defined. Read *et al.* (1990) use the following amusing example to illustrate goal-derived categories: 'the items wedding pictures, stereo and children are not physically similar to one another, yet they hang together as members of the goal-derived category "things to take out of the house in case of a fire"' (1990: 1048). In deciding which behaviours should belong under particular trait categories, psychologists and laypeople therefore have either of the above cognitive strategies at their disposal.

Importantly, Read *et al.* (1990) found that both typicality and goal-relatedness played a role in the perceived coherence of personality traits. They suggest that we may use either a taxonomic categorisation (family resemblance or typicality) or goal-derived categories in deciding which behaviours belong together under different personality trait labels. This suggests that personality traits or dispositions may reflect goals which behaviours have in common. However, it may still be the case that not all traits are goal-based categories. Read *et al.* suggest that some interpersonal traits, such as 'gregariousness', may reflect the goals of wanting to be with people or being liked, in which case the behaviour and thoughts of a gregarious person may be energised by plans for achieving those goals and may have associated with the trait various beliefs about people and situations, which are consistent with those goals. However, they acknowledge that other traits may involve a set of beliefs, rather than goal-directed plans of action. For example, the trait locus of control may reflect a belief about the causes of outcomes, rather than underlying goals for future action.

Understanding the cognitive basis of trait-based categories may, therefore, help us to identify which individual differences in behaviour and thought are a function of underlying goals and which individual differences are governed by other factors such as beliefs or attitudes. Research on how we cognitively categorise information about thoughts and behaviour suggests that 'personality' may not be a unitary phenomenon. When we talk about 'personality', some of the time we may be referring to clusters of behaviours and thought which are organised around goals for future action, whereas at other times we may be referring to behaviours and thoughts which have a different basis in beliefs, attitudes or other predispositions we have yet to identify precisely.

Goals or temperaments: implications for understanding the causes of individual differences

If we assume that the term 'personality' may refer to either goal-based categories or 'something else', what might that 'something else' be? Can we distinguish between goals as energisers for thoughts and actions and other causes of thought and action? One possible distinction is that goals are cognitive constructs whereas dispositions are affective constructs (to do with our emotions or feelings). Many psychologists have suggested that what we feel and what we think are not always the same thing (Rosenberg and Hovland, 1960). For example, we are all familiar with the popular phrase 'letting your heart rule your head'. One possibility, therefore, is that human behaviour and thought can be determined at times by our **cognition** (what we know), at times by our **affect** (what we feel). This raises the possibility that whereas some of our behaviours and thoughts are organised around cognitive goals and hang together under goal-based personality traits, other behaviours are organised around emotions or feelings. If this is true, then perhaps we may be able to distinguish empirically between the cognitive and affective components of personality.

For instance, personality traits based on affect might be amenable to alteration by drugs because affect may have a physiological basis (our emotions are under the influence of hormones which determine how we feel). On the other hand, traits based on cognitive goal-related behaviours might only be amenable to change using cognitive methods such as psychoanalytic, counselling or other forms of therapy. However, the evidence suggests that it is very difficult to distinguish the effects of affect from cognition. Many studies suggest that what we know about a situation can determine how we label our feelings in the same situation. For example, Schacter and Singer (1962) found that people described their feelings differently after taking a placebo pill (a tablet which had no particular physiological effects) in accordance with how they were led to believe the pill would make them feel. And psychopathologies such as depression which clearly represent disturbances to people's affective or emotional behaviour, and can be treated successfully with anti-depressant drugs, may also be treated successfully using cognitive-behavioural interventions. Another possible way of distinguishing between affective and cognitive behaviours or traits is to assume that whereas we may be born with different levels of emotionality, the goals to which we aspire only emerge later on in life. Thus differences in behaviour which emerge at or shortly after birth may represent affective dispositions distinct from cognitive goal-based traits which appear relatively later in human development. However, although some psychologists have described individual differences in activity levels in babies (Korner, 1973), the fact that very young infants have a very limited repertoire of behaviours anyway means that we cannot easily relate differences in activity at an early age to clusters of behaviour later in life. Nevertheless, some psychologists have shown that early differences may have consequences for individual differences later on in life (Thomas and Chess, 1977; Riese, 1987).

The future of personality

It seems that we may still have to resolve most of the time-honoured issues in the study of personality and individual differences. Like Aristotle, Plato and Galen, we are still trying to understand the relative contributions of nature or nurture and mind and body to human individual differences, and the best ways of predicting how people will respond in various situations. However, more recent research into individual differences suggests that it may be more fruitful to pursue an eclectic approach, integrating theories, research and methods from many different areas of psychology. Hopefully, it has been shown how the integration of research from personality psychology and cognitive psychology may lead the way in this respect.

Summary

In this final chapter, it was suggested that whereas some aspects of personality may be described as differences in temperament, other aspects of personality may have a cognitive basis in the goals which people set themselves and to which they aspire. The identification of which behaviours, perceptions and thoughts have a basis in underlying temperaments and dispositions, and which have a basis in cognitions, is therefore likely to be the greatest challenge which psychologists studying individual differences will have to face in the future. To this end, an integration of research from personality psychology and cognitive psychology is most likely to provide the best way forward.

Further reading

Read, S.J., Jones, D.K. and Miller, L.C. (1990). Traits as goal-based categories: the importance of goals in the coherence of dispositional categories. *Journal of Personality and Social Psychology*, 58, 6, 1048–1061. This journal article is not too difficult to read and presents evidence which suggests that many personality traits may be goal-based. It also discusses the implications of this for the future of personality psychology and individual differences.

Glossary

The first occurrence of each of these terms is high-lighted in **bold** type in the main text.

actor-observer divergence Effect observed in experiments on attribution whereby participants in a situation (actors) and onlookers (observers) make different attributional judgements about the causes of an event.

affect Mood, emotion or feelings. Often contrasted with cognition (knowledge or intellect).

aggregation Method for establishing the cross-situational consistency of behaviour whereby behaviour is measured over several similar situational contexts over a period of time.

anal stage/anal personality The second of Freud's psychosexual stages in which failure to resolve conflict is assumed to give rise to an anal personality characterised by obstinacy, order-liness and parsimony.

anti-depressants Drugs used to elevate the mood of people diagnosed as suffering from depression.

applied psychology   Refers to any area of psychology which applies psychological knowledge to people's problems in a real-world setting.

associative learning   A simple form of learning whereby two objects or events become connected via conditioning so that the occurrence of one may predict the other.

attitude   A positive or negative evaluation of some object, event or person.

attribution   *See* **causal attribution.**

attributional style questionnaire   A test used to measure whether an individual attributes the causes of events to internal or external, stable or unstable and global or specific factors. Often used with depressed patients.

authoritarian personality   Person who possesses a rigid, conservative personality trait prone to prejudiced attitudes and behaviour, proposed by Adorno.

behavioural control   Refers to the process by which individuals gain command of their actions.

biases   *See* **cognitive bias.**

bystander apathy   The effect in social psychology whereby people in a group are less likely to help a victim than people on their own.

causal attribution   A decision about the causes of behaviour.

classical conditioning   A form of associative learning proposed by Pavlov, in which an unconditioned (or naturally derived) response such as salivation may be elicited by a neutral stimulus, such as a tone, when this has been paired with an unconditioned stimulus of biological importance to the organism, such as food.

client-centred therapy   A type of therapy invented by Carl Rogers, in which the client's present feelings can be acknowledged within a non-judgemental and safe setting.

cognition   Refers to mental processes concerned with thinking and knowledge structures, including memory, attention and problem solving.

cognitive bias   A tendency to over or under value certain types of information when making decisions.

cognitive psychology   The area of psychology concerned with the study of cognition.

cognitive style   A preferred way of using one's cognition or a preference for tackling a problem in a particular way.

cognitive-behavioural intervention   Therapy aimed at altering behaviour by encouraging the client to modify his/her perception of situations, events or the self.

compliance   A change of behaviour after exposure to the opinions of others.

conditionability   Refers to the ease with which one can acquire learned or conditioned associations. *See also* **classical conditioning; operant conditioning.**

conflict   As used in psychoanalytic theories of personality, usually refers to a state whereby a biological impulse conflicts with social acceptability resulting in anxiety and guilt.

conformity   Social influence of the majority on an individual's opinions or behaviour.

consensus   The norm, or tendency of the majority. One of the dimensions which Kelley suggested we use to make attributional judgements of causality.

consistency   Reliability of some event, behaviour or measurement over time or across situations. One of the dimensions which Kelley suggested we use to make attributional judgements of causality.

constructive alternativism   Philosophical tradition which proposes that every individual uniquely reconstructs or re-categorises information about people or events.

correlation   Statistical relationship between two sets of measures expressed quantitatively as a positive or negative figure between +1 and −1.

cortical arousal   The level of electrochemical activity within the cortex of the brain.

costs/benefits   The terms cost and benefit are derived from economics. In cognitive psychology these terms are used to refer to the negative aspects of a situation (costs) and the positive aspects (benefits) which people weigh up when making a decision.

counselling   A collective term for therapies which focus on the client's self-perception.

delayed gratification   The ability to ignore immediately rewarding outcomes in favour of more long term benefits. Used in psychoanalytic psychology to refer specifically to the inhibition of instincts or biological drives until a socially appropriate outlet can be found.

denial   One of Freud's ego defence mechanisms. Failure to face reality when this is too painful to admit to consciousness.

depression   Disturbance of mood resulting in flat affect, inertia and in severe cases withdrawal.

determinism   Philosophical tradition which asserts that what we are and what we do are beyond our control and therefore not our responsibility.

developmental psychology   The area of psychology concerned with how human beings develop from birth to adulthood.

discrimination learning   Term derived from operant conditioning to describe learning to respond to a specific stimulus by reinforcement.

displacement   One of Freud's ego defence mechanisms whereby sexual or aggressive impulses can be redirected onto a less threatening object.

disposition   An enduring, stable tendency which qualifies a person.

distinctiveness   One of Harold Kelley's dimensions which people use to make attributional judgements of causality. Distinctive behaviour is behaviour which is evident only in relation to a specific object or situation. This use of the term differs from its everyday meaning of 'unusual'.

dogmatism   The tendency to dislike new ideas. A social-cognitive style proposed by Rokeach, assumed to arise from a particular way of organising social information in cognition.

dualism   The philosophical distinction drawn between 'mind' or incorporeal aspects of being and 'body' or corporeal aspects of being.

ego   The hypothetical construct proposed by Freud which mediates between the instinctual demands of the *id* and the reality of the social environment.

ego defence mechanism   In psychoanalytic psychology, strategies for diverting the sexual and aggressive impulses of the *id*, so as to reduce sexual and aggressive tension.

epigenetic principle   Term coined by Erikson to describe the process by which humans develop through the resolution of social conflicts at genetically determined maturational stages.

eros   The name given by Freud to label sexual instincts.

expectancies   Term used by Bandura to refer to implicit predictions about the likelihood of being reinforced or punished for a behaviour.

explicit   Used in psychology to refer to phenomena which are directly observable (opposite of implicit).

extinction   The decrease in responses to a preconditioning level when reinforcement is withheld.

extroversion/introversion   One of Eysenck's personality dimensions. Extroverts are sociable, impulsive and seek stimulation whereas introverts are quiet, unsociable and avoid stimulation.

factor   *See* **factor analysis**.

factor analysis   A statistical procedure for identifying clusters of related traits or behavioural responses (factors). Factors are assumed to underlie basic personality traits and are thus the quantitative basis for trait theories of personality.

feedback   The monitoring of responses with a view to evaluating their effectiveness in bringing about a particular outcome or goal state.

field dependence/independence   A dimension which taps alternative strategies for processing perceptual or social information by reliance on either internal cues (field independent style) or external cues (field dependent style).

fixation   Psychoanalytic term which refers to the process by which development may become partly arrested (or fixated) at one of Freud's psycho-sexual stages.

fragmentation   According to Yochelson and Samenow's theory of criminality, fragmentation is the ability present in criminals to dissociate their criminal acts from their expressed morality.

free will   The capacity to influence and control one's character and behaviour (opposite of determinism).

frontal lobes   The structures at the front of the brain thought to be involved in planning and executing complex behaviour.

Fundamental Attribution Error   The tendency to blame people for their actions and ignore situational determinants of behaviour when making attributional judgements of causality.

general intelligence factor   A factor identified by Spearman which taps general intellectual ability and which is assumed to underlie all forms of thinking and adaptive behaviour. *See also* **factor analysis**.

generalisation   Conditioning term which means responding in the same way to similar objects or stimuli.

Gestalt psychology   The school in psychology which asserts that 'the whole is greater than the sum of parts'. Today, its main influence is to be found in psychological theories which emphasise the whole person, and which prefer a holistic (non-reductionist) approach to the study of human nature.

goals   A goal refers to some desired outcome or end state which the individual or organism strives to achieve.

heuristic   A short cut or strategy which people use in making decisions.

humanist   Adherant to the phenomenological school in psychology which emphasises people's unique experiences and perceptions of the self.

humours   Body fluids assumed by early psychologists and philosophers to influence personality or temperament.

id   An unconscious construct consisting of instincts and biological drives assumed by Freud to direct most of human behaviour and thought.

ideal self   The type of person we aspire to be. According to Rogers, our ideal self may be either consistent or inconsistent with our self-concept.

identification   Originally a psychoanalytic term, now widely used in psychology to refer to the process whereby a child takes on the characteristics of or emulates the behaviours of someone whom it admires and is close to.

identity crisis   According to Erikson, the point in psycho-social development at which the adolescent experiences conflict about his/her identity.

ideographic   Applies to those approaches in personality psychology which focus on individual uniqueness rather than group differences.

implicit   Used in psychology to refer to phenomena which are discreet or not directly observable, such as thought processes or memory (opposite of explicit).

impression-formation   The process by which we form attitudes about the characteristics of people and their behaviour.

impulsiveness   The tendency to act without thinking about the possible consequences.

information processing   A term derived from information technology. Used in psychology to describe how people encode, store and retrieve information when solving problems in a way analogous to computers.

inhibition/disinhibition   As used by social-learning theorists such as Bandura, inhibition refers to the exercise of restraint over behaviour when this is unlikely to lead to reinforcement, or when this may have negative consequences. Disinhibition is the opposite process, and refers to the process whereby a behaviour is carried out in order to gain reinforcement.

innate   Genetically pre-programmed.

instincts   Basic biological drives which motivate human and animal behaviour.

interactionism   The approach to personality psychology which argues that personality dispositions and situations exert a mutual influence on behaviour.

interference A cognitive psychological term used to describe the inappropriate intrusion of information stored in memory into some current information processing task resulting in a disruption to performance.

introspection A psychological method in which people are asked to reflect on and report their inner experiences.

locus of control A trait proposed by Rotter which measures the extent to which individuals perceive that events which happen in their lives are caused by internal factors (something to do with themselves) or external factors (outside influences beyond their control).

Matching Familiar Figures Test A cognitive figure-matching task used by Kagan to measure the cognitive trait of reflection-impulsivity in children.

mind/body problem The philosophical question which askes whether mind or body should be considered the most important aspect of 'being'. *See also* **dualism.**

modelling A form of observational learning in which observed behaviour is reproduced in order to bring about reinforcement.

nature In psychology the term nature is used to refer to the influence of genetic predispositions or biologically inherited characteristics present at birth on people's characters or behaviour.

negative reinforcement The reinforcing effects of removing an aversive/undesirable stimulus or situation. For instance, in conditioning trials being given the opportunity to operate a lever which switches off electric shocks may be used as a reinforcer.

neuroses Anxiety related disorders.

neuroticism/stability One of the personality trait dimensions proposed by Eysenck. Whereas neurotic individuals are emotionally reactive, stable individuals are emotionally stable.

nomothetic Describes the approach to personality psychology which attempts to identify personality dimensions which can be quantified and used to compare groups of individuals.

nurture The effects of upbringing or the environment from birth onwards.

obedience Following an order given by someone in a position of authority.

observational learning The process of learning through observation of a live model or a symbolic one (such as one presented in the media).

Oedipal personality According to Freud, this personality type arises from fixation at the phallic stage when the male child experiences desire for his mother and hostility towards his father.

operant conditioning A form of associative learning. The increase in the frequency of a behavioural response following reinforcement.

oral stage/personality The oral stage is the first of Freud's psycho-sexual stages when sexual energy is centred around the mouth. 'Fixation' at this stage gives rise to an oral personality who is over-trusting and dependent.

organismic valuing process According to Rogers, the basic need which all humans have to be unconditionally loved and highly regarded by others.

peer ratings Psychometric data based on the evaluation of an individual's personality by his/her acquaintances or friends.

perception The process of registering and interpreting information from the sensory system.

persecutory delusions Feelings of paranoia in which the person becomes convinced that some other person or being means to cause them harm.

perseveration Stereotypic repetition of actions.

personal construct According to George Kelly, individual patterns or templates which we use to make sense of the world.

phallic stage *See* **Oedipal personality**.

phenomenology The approach in psychology which emphasises people's unique experiences.

placebo A treatment which has no known physiological effects but which nevertheless brings about an improvement in a patient's medical or psychological condition.

priming The phenomenon whereby something presented in a previous trial or context exerts an influence over future behaviour.

probability The mathematical method for predicting the likelihood of future events.

projection One of Freud's ego defence mechanisms which involves attributing one's own unacceptable impulses to other people. According to Freud projection formed the basis for prejudiced attitudes.

prototype A best example of some category of objects.

psychoanalysis A form of therapy invented by Freud in which clients are encouraged to air unconscious feelings and early childhood experiences to relieve anxiety and conflict.

psychometric method   Method for quantifying psychological qualities.

psychopathology   Psychological disturbance or mental illness.

psychopharmacology   The study of the effects of drugs on behaviour.

psycho-sexual theory   Term used by Freud to label his theory of personality development which is based on sexual conflict at various stages in childhood.

psychosomatic   Describes any physical symptoms of ill-health for which there is no obvious physical or physiological cause.

psychoticism   One of Eysenck's personality trait dimensions which taps unconventional behaviour, a tendency not to obey authority and a susceptibility to mental illness.

punishment   In conditioning, any consequence of behaviour which decreases the likelihood of the response being repeated.

rationalisation   A psychoanalytic defence mechanism. Distorting reality to bolster your own self-esteem.

reaction formation   Expressing attitudes which conflict with your emotions. One of the ego defence mechanisms proposed by Freud.

reductionism   The view that human nature can best be understood by studying its component parts.

reflection-impulsivity   The cognitive trait related to impulsiveness proposed by Kagan which is measured by responses on the Matching Familiar Figures Test. Slow and accurate responses are reflective and fast and inaccurate responses are impulsive. *See also* **Matching Familiar Figures Test.**

reinforcement   Any consequence that increases the likelihood that a response will be repeated.

repression   The major ego defence mechanism proposed by Freud whereby unacceptable or anxiety provoking thoughts are pushed out of awareness.

schema   Set of cognitions that arise from past experiences which guide the processing of new information.

script   Cognitions about what to expect in certain sorts of situation based on past experience which influence behaviour whenever a similar situation is encountered in future.

self-actualisation   The pinnacle of Maslow's hierarchy of needs. According to Maslow, the self-actualised person has an efficient perception of reality, is accepting of others, is spontaneous, creative, has a sense of humour, is democratic, autonomous and has peak experiences.

self-concept   Our perception of what we are like, our sense of self.

self-esteem   An individual's sense of self-worth. Self-esteem as a personality dimension measures the extent to which a person values or undervalues themselves.

self-report   Psychometric data based on individuals' reports of their own behaviour, thoughts or feelings.

self-serving bias   The tendency to attribute positive outcomes to internal factors (things about the self) and negative outcomes to external factors (situations or chance events).

shaping   The building up of chains of responses through reinforcement of appropriate behaviours.

situationism   The view in psychology that all human behaviour is determined by situations or external events.

social-cognition   The area of psychology which is concerned with the study of people's thought processes and decision making in a social context.

social influence   The effects of the presence of other people on behaviour.

social-learning   Approach to personality psychology which argues that people learn behaviour in a social setting via observational learning and modelling.

stereotype   An abstract representation of the characteristics of a social group.

stimulus   Some aspect of the experimental environment which elicits a reaction or response.

strategy   A set of plans which are designed to achieve some end or goal.

sub-goal   Subordinate category of goal. *See also* **goals**.

sublimation   Psychoanalytic defence mechanism whereby sexual or aggressive energy can be diverted into healthy activities such as work or artistic pursuits.

superego   According to Freud, the part of the human psyche which strives for moral perfection and which internalises society's standards.

tabula rasa   Latin for 'blank slate'. Used by the behaviourists to describe the state of the infant at birth.

temperament   An individual's characteristic mood, activity level or sensitivity to stimulation.

thanatos   Collective term used by Freud to label death or aggressive instincts.

threshold   The transitional point at which a stimulus or difference between two stimuli not previously perceived becomes perceptible.

trait   An enduring characteristic or dimension of personality which can be measured and according to which an individual's personality can be described and compared with others.

unconditional positive regard   According to Rogers, the type of unconditional love or respect which does not depend on reciprocity, such as the ideal of love between a mother and her child. According to Rogers all children need unconditional positive regard from their parents but rarely get this.

References

Abramson, L.Y., Seligman, M.E.P and Teasdale, J.D. (1978). Learned helplessness in humans: critique and reformulation. *Journal of Abnormal Psychology*, 78, 40–74.

Adorno, T.W., Frenkel-Brunswick, E., Levinson, D.J. and Sanford, R.N. (1950). *The Authoritarian Personality*. New York: Harper & Row.

Ajzen, I. (1988). *Attitudes, Personality and Behaviour*. Chicago: Dorsey Press.

Allport, G.W. (1937). *Personality: a psychological interpretation*. New York: Holt, Rinehart, Winston.

Allport, G.W. (1961). *Pattern and Growth in Personality*. New York: Holt, Rinehart, Winston.

Aristotle (1984). Nichomachaen Ethics V, in B.J. Barnes (ed.), *The Complete Works of Aristotle*. Guilford: Princeton University Press.

Aronson, E. (1984). *The Social Animal*. 4th edn. New York: W.H. Freeman and Co.

Asch, S. (1946). Forming impressions of personality. *Journal of Abnormal and Social Psychology*, 41, 258–290.

Asch, S. (1956). Studies of independence and conformity: a minority of one against a unanimous majority. *Psychological Monographs*, 70(9), 416.

Bandura, A. (1977). *Social Learning Theory*. Englewood Cliffs, N.J.: Prentice Hall.

Bandura, A. and Walters, R.H. (1963). *Social Learning and Personality Development*. New York: Holt Rinehart Winston.

Bandura, A., Ross, D. and Ross, S.A. (1961). Transmission of aggression through imitation of aggressive models. *Journal of Abnormal and Social Psychology*, 63(3), 575–582.

Baron J.B. (1995). *Thinking and Deciding*. Cambridge: Cambridge University Press.

Beardslee, D.C. and Wertheimer, M. (1958). (English part-translation), in *Readings in Perception*, Princeton: Princeton University Press, pp. 115–135.

Beck, S.J. and Ollendick, T.H. (1976). Personal space, sex of experimenter and locus of control in normal and delinquent adolescents. *Psychological Reports*, 38, 383–387.

Bentall, R.P., commentary in Deary, I.J. and Matthews, G. (1993). Personality traits are alive and well. *The Psychologist*. July. British Psychological Society.

Blass, T. (1991). Understanding behaviour in the Milgram Obedience Experiment: the role of personality, situations and their interactions. *Journal of Personality and Social Psychology*, 60(3), 398–413.

Bowers, K.S. (1973). Situationism in psychology. An analysis and a critique. *Psychological Review*, 80(5), 307–336.

Brewin, C. (1988). *Cognitive Foundations of Clinical Psychology*. Hove, Sussex: Erlbaum.

Brunas-Wagstaff, J., Bergquist, A. and Wagstaff, G.F. (1994). Cognitive correlates of functional and dysfunctional impulsivity. *Personality and Individual Differences*, 17(2), 289–292.

Byrne, D. (1961). The repression-sensitization scale: rationale, reliability and validity. *Journal of Personality*, 29, 33–39.

Carver, C.S. and Scheier, M.F. (1992). *Perspectives on Personality*. Boston: Allyn & Bacon.

Cattell, R.B. (1965). *The Scientific Analysis of Personality*. Baltimore: Penguin Books.

Chandler, M.J. (1973). Egocentrism and anti-social behaviour: the assessment and training of social perspective taking skills. *Developmental Psychology*, 9, 326–332.

Dickman, S.J. (1990). Functional and dysfunctional impulsivity: personality and cognitive correlates. *Journal of Personality and Social Psychology*, 58(1), 95–102.

Eiser, J.R. and Van der Pligt, J. (1988). *Attitudes and Decisions*. New Essential Psychology Series. London: Routledge.

Elms, A.C. and Milgram, S. (1966). Personality characteristics associated with obedience and defiance toward authoritative command. *Journal of Experimental Research in Psychology*, 1, 282–289.

Epstein, S. (1977). Traits are alive and well, in D. Magnusson and N. Endler (eds), *Personality at the Crossroads: Current Issues in Interactional Psychology*. Hillsdale NJ: Erlbaun.

Epstein, S. (1979). The stability of behaviour. I. On predicting most of the people much of the time. *Journal of Personality and Social Psychology*, 37, 1097–1126.

Epstein, S. (1983). Aggregation and beyond: some basic issues on the prediction of behaviour. *Journal of Personality*, 51, 360–392.

Erikson, E. (1963). *Childhood and Society*. New York: Norton. (Originally published in 1950.)

Eysenck, H.J. (1970). *The Structure of Human Personality*. 3rd edn. London: Methuen.

Eysenck, H.J. (1986). *Decline and Fall of the Freudian Empire*. London: Pelican.

Eysenck, H.J. and Levey, A. (1972). Conditioning, introversion-extraversion, and the strength of the nervous system, in V.B. Nebylitsyn and J.A. Gray (eds), *The Biological Bases of Individual Behaviour*, London: Academic Press.

Eysenck, H.J., Arnold, W.J. and Meili, R. (1975). *Encyclopedia of Psychology*. Volume 1 (A–K). Volume 2 (L–Z). London: Fontana.

Freedman, B.J., Rosenthal, L., Donahoe, C.P., Schlundt, D.G. and McFall, R.M. (1978). A social-behavioural analysis of skills deficits in delinquent and non-delinquent adolescent boys. *Journal of Consulting and Clinical Psychology*, 46(1), 448–462.

Freud, A. (1966). *The Ego and the Mechanisms of Defense*. (Revised edn). New York: International Universities Press.

Freud, S. (1933). *New Introductory Lectures on Psychoanalysis*. (Revised edn). New York: Norton. (Translated by W.J.H. Sprott.)

Freud, S. (1953). Three essays in sexuality, in J. Strachey (ed.), *The Standard Edition of the Complete Psychological Works of Sigmund Freud*, vol. 7. London: Hogarth Press. (Originally published l905.)

Freud, S. (1962). *The Ego and the Id*. New York: Norton. (Originally published 1923.)

Gray, J.A. (1981). A critique of Eysenck's theory of personality, in H.J. Eysenck (ed.), *A Model for Personality*. Berlin: Springer-Verlag.

Gregorc, A. (1985). *Inside Styles: beyond the basics*. Maynard, MA: Gabriel Systems.

Gregory, R.L. (1987). *The Oxford Companion to the Mind*. Oxford: Oxford University Press.

Hall, V. and Russell, W. (1974). Multitrait-multimethod analysis of conceptual tempo. *Journal of Educational Psychology*, 66, 932–939.

Hampson, S.E. (1988). *The Construction of Personality. An Introduction*. London: Routledge.

Hartshorne, H. and May, A. (1928). *Studies in the Nature of Character*. Vol. I. *Studies in Deceit*. New York: Macmillian.

Heider, F. (1958). *The Psychology of Interpersonal Relations*. New York: Wiley.

Hjelle, L.A. and Ziegler, D.J. (1981a). Sigmund Freud: a psychoanalytic theory of personality, in *Personality, Basic Theories and Assumptions*. New York: McGraw-Hill.

Hjelle, L.A. and Ziegler, D.J. (1981b). Erik Erikson: a psychosocial theory of personality, in *Personality, Basic Theories and Assumptions*. New York: McGraw-Hill.

Hollin, C. (1989). Understanding crime, in *Psychology and Crime: an introduction to criminological psychology*. London: Routledge, pp. 34–38.

Jamieson, J. (1992). The cognitive styles of reflection-impulsivity and field independence-dependence and ESL success. *The Modern Language Journal*, 76, 491–501.

Jones, E.E. and Davis, K.E. (1965). From acts to dispositions: the attribution process in person perception, in L. Berkowitz (ed.), *Advances in Experimental Social Psychology*, vol. 2. New York: Academic Press.

Jones, E.E. and Nisbett, R.E. (1972). The actor and the observer. Divergent perceptions of the causes of behaviour, in *Attribution: perceiving the causes of behaviour*. Morristown, NJ: General Learning Press.

Kagan, J. (1965). Impulsive and reflective children: significance of conceptual tempo, in J. Krumboltz (ed.), *Learning and the Educational Process*. Chicago IL: Rand McNally.

Kagan, J. (1981). *The Second Year: the emergence of self-awareness*. Cambridge, MA: Harvard University Press.

Kahneman, D. and Tversky, A. (1972). Subjective probability: a judgement of representativeness. *Cognitive Psychology*, 3, 430–454.

Kahneman, D. and Tversky, A. (1979). Prospect theory: an analysis of decisions under risk. *Econometrica*, 47, 263–291.

Kaney, S. and Bentall, R.P. (1989). Persecutory delusions and attributional style. *British Journal of Medical Psychology*, 62, 191–198.

Kelley, H.H. (1973). The process of causal attribution. *American Psychologist*, 28, 107–128.

Kelly, G.A. (1955). *The Psychology of Personal Constructs*, vols 1 and 2. New York: Norton.

Kenrick, D.T., McCreath, H.E., Govern, J., King, R. and Bordin, J. (1990). Person–environment intersections: everyday settings and common trait dimensions. *Journal of Personality and Social Psychology*, 58(4), 685–698.

Kline, P. (1984). Psychology and Freudian Theory. London and New York: Methuen.

Kline, P. (1994). *An Easy Guide to Factor Analysis*. London: Routledge.

Kopp, C.B. (1982). Antecedents of self-regulation: a developmental perspective. *Developmental Psychology*, 18, 199–214.

Korner, A.F. (1973). Individual differences at birth: implications for early experience and later development, in J.C. Westman (ed.), *Individual Differences in Children*. New York: Wiley.

Kretschmer, E. (1925). *Physique and Character*. 2nd edn. New York: Harcourt, Brace, Jovanovich.

Kuczynski, L. and Kochanska, G. (1990). Development of children's noncompliance strategies from toddlerhood to age five. *Developmental Psychology*, 26, 398–408.

Kumchy, C. and Sayer, L.A. (1980). Locus of control and delinquent adolescent populations. *Psychological Reports*, 46(1), 307–310.

Langer, E.J. (1975). The illusion of control. *Journal of Personality and Social Psychology*, 32, 311–328.

McArthur, L.Z. (1972). The how and what of why: some determinants and consequences of causal attribution. *Journal of Personality and Social Psychology*, 22, 171–193.

157

McConnell, J.V. (1974). *Understanding Human Behavior*. New York: Holt, Rinehart, Winston.

McCrae, R.R. and Costa, P.T. Jr (1987). Validation of the five-factor model of personality across instruments and observers. *Journal of Personality and Social Psychology*, 52, 81–90.

Marton, F. and Saljo, R. (1976). On qualitative differences in learning: 1: Outcome and process. *British Journal of Educational Psychology*, 46, 4–11.

Marton, F., Mounsell, D. and Entwhistle, N. (eds) (1984). *The Experience of Learning*. Edinburgh: Scottish Academic Press.

Maslow, A.H. (1970). *Motivation and Personality*. New York: Harper & Row.

Messer, S.B. (1970). Reflection-impulsivity. Stability and school failure. *Journal of Educational Psychology*, 61, 487–490.

Milgram, S. (1963). Behavioural study of obedience. *Journal of Abnormal and Social Psychology*, 67, 371–378.

Milgram, S. (1965). Some conditions of obedience and disobedience to authority. *Human Relations*, 18, 57–76.

Miller, C.M.L. and Parlett, M. (1974). *Up to the Mark. A Study of the Examination Game*. Guildford: S.R.H.E.

Mischel, W. (1968). *Personality and Assessment*. New York: Wiley.

Mischel, W. (1969). Continuity and change in personality. *American Psychologist*, 24, 1012–1018.

Mischel, W. and Peake, P.K. (1982). In search of consistency: measure for measure, in M.P. Zanna, E.T. Higgins and C.P. Herman (eds), Consistency in Social Behaviour: The Ontario Symposium.Vol. 2. Hillsdale, NJ: Erlbaum.

Monsell, S. (1996). Control of mental processes, in V. Bruce (ed.), *Unsolved Mysteries of the Mind: tutorial essays in cognition*. London: Erlbaum and Hove: Taylor and Francis.

Nisbett, R.E. and Borgida, E. (1975). Attribution and the psychology of prediction. *Journal of Personality and Social Psychology*, 32, 932–943.

Nisbett, R.E. and Ross, L. (1980). *Human Inference: strategies and shortcomings of social judgement*. Englewood Cliffs, NJ: Prentice Hall.

Norman, D.A. (1981). Categorisation of action slips. *Psychological Review*, 88, 1–15.

Norton, L.S. and Crowley, C.M. (1995). Can students be helped to learn how to learn? An evaluation of an approach to learning programme for first year degree students. *Higher Education*, 29, 307–328.

Norton, L.S., Dickins, T.E. and McLaughlin-Cook, N. (1996). Rules of the game in essay writing. *Psychology Teaching Review*, 5, 1–14.

Pavlov, I.P. (1927). *Conditioned Reflexes*. New York: Oxford University Press.

Plato (1987). *The Republic*. (Translated by D. Lee). Harmondsworth: Penguin.

Plomin, R.A. (1976). Extraversion, sociability and impulsivity. *Journal of Personality Assessment*, 40, 24–30.

Read, S.J., Jones, D.K. and Miller, L.C. (1990). Traits as goal-based categories: the importance of goals in the coherence of dispositional categories. *Journal of Personality and Social Psychology*, 58(6), 1048–1061.

Reason, J.T. (1990). *Human Error*. Cambridge: Cambridge University Press.

Renzulli, J. and Smith, L. (1978). *Learning Styles Inventory*. Mansfield Center, CT: Creative Learning Press.

Riese, M.L. (1987). Temperament stability between the neonatal period and 24 months. *Developmental Psychology*, 23, 216–222.

Rogers, C.R. (1959). A theory of therapy, personality and interpersonal relationships as developed in the client-centred framework, in S. Koch (ed.), *Psychology: a study of a science*, vol. 3. New York: McGraw-Hill.

Rogers, C. and Dymond, R. (eds) (1954). *Psychotherapy and Personality Change*. Chicago: University of Chicago Press.

Rokeach, M. (1954). The nature and meaning of dogmatism. *Psychological Review*, 61, 194–204.

Rosenberg, M.J. and Hovland, C.I. (1960). Cognitive, affective and behavioural components of attitudes, in M.J. Rosenberg, C.I. Hovland, W.J. McGuire, R.P. Abelson and J.W. Brehm (eds), *Attitude Organisation and Change: an analysis of consistency among attitude components*. New Haven, CN: Yale University Press.

Ross, R.R. and Fabiano, E.A. (1985). *Time to Think: a cognitive model of delinquency prevention and offender rehabilitation*. Johnson City, Tenn: Institute of Social Sciences and Arts.

Rotter, J.B. (1966). Generalised expectancies for internal versus external control of reinforcement. *Psychological Monographs*, 80, no. 609.

Schacter, S. and Singer, J.E. (1962). Cognitive, social and physiological determinants of emotional state. *Psychological Review*, 69, 379–399.

Schaffer, R.H. (1996). *Social Development*. Cambridge, MA and Oxford: Blackwell.

Schank, R.C. and Abelson, R.P. (1977). *Scripts, Plans, Goals and Understanding*. Hillsdale NJ: Erlbaum.

Sheldon, W.H. (1942). *The Varieties of Temperament*. New York: Harper & Row.

Sheldon, W.H., Stevens, S.S. and Tucker, W.B. (1940). *The Varieties of Human Physique*. New York: Harper & Row.

Simon, H.A. (1957). *Models of Man: social and rational*. New York: Wiley.

Simon, H.A. (1967). Motivational and emotional controls of cognition. *Psychological Review*, 74, 29–39.

Skinner, B.F. (1938). *The Behaviour of Organisms*. New York: Appleton-Century-Crofts.

Skinner, B.F. (1971). *Beyond Freedom and Dignity*. New York: Knopf.

Smedslund, J. (1963). The concept of correlation in adults. *Scandinavian Journal of Psychology*, 4, 165–173.

Spearman, C. (1904). 'General intelligence' objectively determined and measured. *American Journal of Psychology*, 15, 201–293.

Stephenson, W. (1953). *The Study of Behavior: Q-technique and its methodology*. Chicago: Chicago University Press.

Sternberg, R.J. (1988). Mental self-government: a theory of intellectual styles and their development. *Human Development*, 31, 197–224.

Sternberg, R.J. (1995). Intelligence and cognitive styles, in Hampson, S.E. and Colman, A.M. (eds), *Individual Differences and Personality*. Essential Psychology series. London and New York: Longman.

Stevens, R. (1983). *Freud and Psychoanalysis: an exposition and appraisal*. Milton Keynes: Open University Press.

Storr, A. (1970). *Human Aggression*. Harmondsworth: Penguin.

Svensson, L. (1977). On qualitative differences in learning: III. Study skill and learning. *British Journal of Educational Psychology*, 47, 233–243.

Thomas, A. and Chess, S. (1977). *Temperament and Development*. New York: Brunner/Mazel.

Turiel, E. (1983). *The Development of Social Knowledge: morality and convention*. Cambridge: Cambridge University Press.

Watson, J.B. and Raynor, R. (1920). Conditioned Emotional Reactions. *Journal of Experimental Psychology*, 3, 1–14.

Wells, G.L. and Harvey, J.H. (1977). Do people use consensus information in making causal attributions? *Journal of Personality and Social Psychology*, 35, 279–293.

Witkin, H.A., Lewis, H.B., Hertzman, M., Machover, K., Meissner, P.B. and Wapner, S. (1954). *Personality Through Perception*. New York: Harper.

Yochelson, S. and Samenow, S.E. (1976). *The Criminal Personality: a profile for change*, vol. l. New York: Jason Aronsen.

Zebrowitz, L.A. (1990). *Social Perception*. Milton Keynes: Open University Press.

Zuckerman, M. (1979). Attribution of success and failure revisited, or: the motivational bias is alive and well in attribution theory. *Journal of Personality*, 47, 245–287.

Index